Dear David,

a lot of practice to have written this book. Keep moving forward. The examined life is worth the effort.

Cheers, Jsl

PRAISE FOR
ALIGNMENT STRONG

"This is a vital handbook for any company CEO, president, owner, business leader, or employee wishing to grow. It is down to earth and personal and possesses some amazing tools for assessing one's self or an organization. *Alignment Strong* is a valuable resource for our worldwide 26,000 Vistage members. The application of this book will increase the effectiveness of their roles and enhance their lives."

—Richard Beadle, founder, Vistage Michigan

"Our closely held international freight forwarding/logistics company engaged John while he was in graduate school. While the performance of our company was acceptable, we needed help in order to survive in an increasingly competitive global industry. A fifteen-year engagement (three successive five-year strategic visions) resulted. The Alignment Strong model shaped our company to strategically "out-compete" our much larger global rivals. Values, culture, strategic vision, and employee engagement were foundational. A "talking stick" was carved out of a tree branch and frequently used at our team retreats to reinforce a culture of openness and trust between our American, European, Asia/Australia, and Latin American operation teams, using the Alignment Strong framework. We achieved significant growth in revenue and profitability, while developing long-term employee satisfaction. The Alignment Strong model helped us to re-vision, further build, and sustain our company's competitive posture."

—Joe Coughlin, CEO, F.X. Coughlin Company

"Almost twenty years ago, we were a $5 million company. Things were going well, but we weren't growing to the next level. I met John and he began introducing me to some of the components that now fill the pages of this book. Our culture changed, our team began to get real with each other, and we pushed beyond the plateau. Challenged and encouraged by John's coaching, we more than tripled the size of our business."

—**Mike Mancinelli, founder and CEO, Great Lakes Woodworking**

"Our firm has worked with John for over half a decade. The guidance and facilitation he has provided to us are key factors in our success. His knowledge and study of organizational design and dynamics are based on empirical research; his ability to facilitate and bridge understandings is possible only due to the massive amount of work he has dedicated to himself and his clients. This book gives readers a glimpse into the process he facilitates with his clients. If your organization is seeking a model to align the team and build trust, look no further."

—**Todd Hohauser, CEO, FEA, Harvey Hohauser & Associates, and Global Chair, IIC Partners**

"In today's business world, change is not only a constant—it's an accelerating challenge that requires leaders' attention and requires all employees' skills to be sharpened and attention-focused. *Alignment Strong* is a must-read for all middle market business owners/managers that seek to recognize and harness their organization's competitive advantage. My president went through the Alignment Strong coaching curriculum. She describes it as receiving an MBA on steroids!"

—**Dan Ponder, CEO, FRANCO**

"Douglas Electric was founded in 1975 by my father. I took over the company in the late '90s. We did not have a complete change framework for the trajectory we desired for growth in people, revenue, and profit. Now we have grown the company to $10 million. John has worked with us, through the COVID-19 pandemic, using Alignment Strong as our cornerstone. I can build from what my father left me, yet have my own imprint in the company culture, what I believe is both strong yet nurturing and yes, more balanced. As a female CEO in a predominantly male industry, I feel a stronger resolve, more self-respect, and quiet determination."

—**Paige Levy, owner and CEO, Douglas Electric**

"My family was steeped in concrete construction industry knowledge since 1946, yet we never fully understood what it took to step back as owners and realize that we have been toiling with success at growing our enterprise for decades, yet were unprepared for sustainable leadership posture. John introduced my brother, Ray, and me to the ten components of *Alignment Strong*. I explained to him what a plumb line is and how it is used in the construction business. It is now foundational to *Alignment Strong*'s Da Vinci Organizational Code. *Alignment Strong* has aligned our company for leadership posture in our industry. We helped each other."

—**Perry Merlo, a founder and owner, Merlo Construction**

"*Alignment Strong* captures John Quinlan's lifelong professional experiences of demonstrating the coordination of an organization's strategic move forward and robustly involving the management team. *Alignment Strong* is not so much a 'how-to' book, but a 'what-to-expect' book when moving to a higher level of performance, both internally and externally. From my background in public accounting, and as CFO for both private and public companies, I have seen the results of Alignment Strong companies versus companies that have not adopted these ten vital components—the evidence is startling. The research that supports the link between Alignment Strong companies and financial results is significant."

—**Philip Rice, president, Legacy Results, Inc.**

"John Quinlan has distilled his experiences and given us this guide to maintain our own business organization. I connected to the core of what Quinlan has provided us with: a road map to success in building your organization. He breaks it down to ten strategic components and fully takes you through the understandings of what they mean and how to apply them to your organization and to yourself. Integrating his experiences as well as incorporating deep thought leadership research into this book, he gives us our own tool, our own plumb line, to build what we want in our business and be competitive in our leadership and in our business."

—Joe McMillan, CEO, McMillan Business Interiors

ALIGNMENT
STRONG

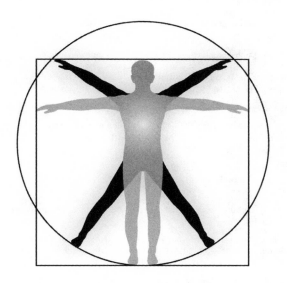

A STRATEGIC and HUMAN-CENTRIC
HANDBOOK for COMPETITIVE LEADERSHIP

JOHN E. QUINLAN

AN INC.
ORIGINAL

An Inc. Original
New York, New York
www.anincoriginal.com

This work is being published under the *An Inc. Original* imprint by an exclusive arrangement with *Inc. Magazine*. *Inc. Magazine* and the *Inc.* logo are registered trademarks of Mansueto Ventures, LLC. The *An Inc. Original* logo is a wholly owned trademark of Mansueto Ventures, LLC.

Distributed by Greenleaf Book Group

For ordering information or special discounts for bulk purchases, please contact Greenleaf Book Group at PO Box 91869, Austin, TX 78709, 512.891.6100.

Design and composition by Greenleaf Book Group
Cover design by Greenleaf Book Group and Kimberly Lance
Getty Images/@iStockphoto.com/kowalska-art

For permission to reproduce copyrighted material, grateful acknowledgment is made to the following:

From "The five keys to a successful Google team" by Julia Rozovsky, Google People Operations, November 17, 2015. https://rework.withgoogle.com/blog/five-keys-to-a-successful-google-team/. All rights reserved.

From *Primal Leadership: Unleashing the Power of Emotional Intelligence* by Daniel Goleman, Richard Boyatzis, and Annie McKee. Copyright © 2013 by Daniel Goleman. Reproduced by permission of Harvard Business School Publishing. All rights reserved.

Publisher's Cataloging-in-Publication data is available.

Print ISBN: 978-1-7334781-7-5

eBook ISBN: 978-1-7334781-8-2

Part of the Tree Neutral® program, which offsets the number of trees consumed in the production and printing of this book by taking proactive steps, such as planting trees in direct proportion to the number of trees used: www.treeneutral.com

TreeNeutral

Printed in the United States of America on acid-free paper

20 21 22 23 24 25   10 9 8 7 6 5 4 3 2 1

First Edition

To my readers, you are the heroes.

*To the writers and teachers who have imparted
their knowledge, you are my pathfinders.*

*To all of the seen and unseen leaders who have
left a footprint, there is no wasted journey.*

"You will need to become vulnerable to what is genuine."
John Quinlan accumulates wisdom on the road.

Contents

FOREWORD

What an honor to write a foreword to *Alignment Strong*, a book that conveys creativity and rigor to important topics such as culture, leadership, strategy, mission efficacy, and individual and organizational performance. As a method, Alignment Strong is a change framework that brings leadership and the science of organization development together, and applies the combination with practicality. Punctuated with personal narratives, business concepts, thought-provoking questions and assessments, this book brings to you, as a leader or leadership candidate, a powerful vantage point on how to view yourself and an organization. I have never read a business text like this before. It integrates the personal and the rational, with an occasional existential nudge to inquiry.

I became engaged in reviewing the author's manuscript from a colleague and thought leader, Bruce L. Gibb, who has a PhD in organizational psychology from the University of Michigan. We both live in Ann Arbor, Michigan. Bruce has known John Quinlan professionally and as a friend for forty years, and he told me that John had returned from Papua New Guinea a few years earlier after building a significant coffee company in a remote rainforest community—and after an assassination attempt on him and his wife. I was interested indeed. I immediately read and thoroughly enjoyed John's first book, *Tau Bada: The Quest and Memoir of a Vulnerable Man*. Also, I viewed the TEDx talk on his vulnerability lessons as a rainforest CEO. I was excited to see what gems his next book would provide.

Alignment Strong propels the organization to a self-sustaining values system, human-centric, technically equipped and postured to compete in today's global community. The change equation is fully explored, as is the role change agents/leaders play in our world today. The book includes terms that are important to know in today's innovation-rich world, with many applications, a case study, reflective analysis sections, and references for further study. From the list of introspective questions for the organization leader to the employee who wants to empower their boss, *Alignment Strong* examines how empowerment and a spirit of inclusion can be incorporated throughout an organization.

John Quinlan's book applies crucially to the business world as well as to nonprofit organizations—and to the classroom. It could supplement our Organization Development and Change curriculum as a textbook at my university. As a business advisor and coach, John reminded me of Jim Collins's bombastic deduction in the first chapter of his book *Good to Great,* emphasizing that a vast majority of companies are good and remain just that. Not great. Yet today, nearly twenty years later, the vast amount of organizations are still sleepwalking. They have adapted to being good, an affliction of satisficing—it is good enough; if it isn't broken, leave it alone— as opposed to achieving their potential and being great.

By following the *Alignment Strong* guide, you can achieve the result of a healthy organization that is both competitively postured and regenerative to sustain itself. John Quinlan individualizes this conversation. He reminded me that the leader becomes the author, the brewmeister, and creates the "change recipe" for his or her enterprise's greatness. Within that change recipe, which will be difficult to replicate by one's rivals, the disease of mediocrity is preventable as well as curable. It is a conscious, curious, and deliberate choice.

Is *Alignment Strong* needed everywhere around the world? Is the need the same in developing countries as developed countries? Is it the same in America as it is in Africa? The same in Australia or Latin

America as in China, Japan, or Russia? It is so compelling to report from our research that the answer is yes! While organizations around the world and throughout the United States may differ culturally, socially, and politically, and life conditions (e.g., poverty, climate, health care, infrastructure, education, water accessibility, income per capita) vary as well, the principles and understandings of *Alignment Strong* apply throughout the world now more than ever. Human nature demands it. Human beings respond to openness, affirmation, trust, and transparency. We need leaders whose goals include continuous wisdom, who are a bit philosophical and certainly transparent, who are not afraid to consistently engage employees and create more leaders at all levels of the organization. I highly recommend that you quietly and reflectively read this book, immediately!

—**Kimberley Barker, PhD**
Director, Institute for Culture and Adaptive Leadership;
Faculty, Eastern Michigan University, Management Department

Motorcycling the Path to Self-Transformation

I am just an ordinary fella, appreciating life, trying to figure things out. In my past life, I was a founder, board chairman, and CEO of a publicly traded company. Then I lost it all after fifteen years of hard work, from my age of twenty-five to forty. My two brothers and I had built a remarkable $430 million financial services company, distributing eleven years of forty-four uninterrupted quarterly cash dividends. My failure as the CEO is the genesis of this book and has been the foundation of my consulting and coaching career. Strategically, I acquired a company that did not align to our existing culture. Personally, I was caught up in the illusions of self-invincibility and self-grandiosity. These two elements, bad strategy and inflated ego, intersected and *poof*, just like that, my organization became extinct. Regretfully, I hurt a lot of people. Scars like these, the inward scars, never disappear. But one can learn from them. Motorcycling remote roads across the United States, a habit I have to this day, helped me to quietly sort things out.

I went back to graduate school to obtain a master of science degree in organizational development. Using what I was taught at school, I became a business consultant and executive coach. Ultimately, I met

Fiona, who became my wife, at a fly-fishing resort, while motorcycling near Crested Butte, Colorado. I asked her if she wanted to go for a ride. What an extreme ride it has been after twenty-one years!

I followed Fiona to Papua New Guinea, where I lived in a remote village, embraced my vulnerability and was nearly assassinated by a clan chief, who was also a close business associate. Fiona and I did build a significant rainforest coffee company. My vulnerability (emotional commitment) became my blind spot. Our success encouraged jealousy and greed from clan chiefs, sorcerers, and politicians. Unknowingly, I was complicit in my own undoing. My ambition to achieve our vision got me into trouble. The illusions of invincibility and willfulness seeped back into my ego. My God, I actually believed I was destined to succeed! Well, "illusion is the first of all pleasures," the philosopher Voltaire offers as consolation. If you want to know more about all that, it's in my first book, *Tau Bada: The Quest and Memoir of a Vulnerable Man*. Yet, both Fiona and I evolved into rainforest entrepreneurs.

Now back in the States, safe from World War II assault rifles, I am, again, a business consultant and executive coach, assisting CEOs to develop strategy and plans by sorting out long-term and short-term priorities and timelines. Within this framework, I also coach the same individuals to potentialize their roles within their organizations as well as to grasp deeper meaning and purpose in their lives. But when I'm off the clock, I embrace reflection and freedom . . . and the open road.

Motorcycling connects me to myself and to others. My inner man and outer man are nudged to oneness. I feel more congruent. It's when I can embrace new ideas and change, both for myself, my family, and my clients. It was on a motorcycle trip that this book crystallized, all from a desert photograph.

On August 8, 2018, Fiona and I departed Detroit, Michigan, for our destination of Phoenix, Arizona. Our journey would cover close to 4,700 miles in twenty-six days, mostly on state highways and county roads.

One particular day, about three weeks into our trip, we found ourselves deep in Monument Valley in Utah, just north of the Arizona state line. Our Navajo guide was showing us a circular, cliff-rock formation known as the Ear of the Wind. The guide suddenly pointed down near my feet. Next to them was a boulder with an *X* carved in its surface. The guide instructed me to place my feet precisely on the marking.

I did so and realized I was in perfect alignment with a weather-bleached pinyon tree and the archway circle in the cliff, carved out by wind and rain over thousands of years, with a backdrop of clear blue sky. The moment was galvanizing. I then hiked down to the tree and spread my arms. I immediately became an essential part of the alignment of the natural landscape in which I was immersed, and Fiona snapped my photo.

When I viewed the photo, I could not see my face in the shadows; my features were indistinguishable. I had become a totemic symbol, descriptive of my own journey and personal alignment. Later, I realized I had mirrored da Vinci's Vitruvian Man. *Fascinating.*

Our Navajo guide exclaimed, "You have no face!" He seemed astonished. But I was not.

I pondered the implications of losing my face as the road lengthened and we continued our journey. My thoughts echoed the author Robert Pirsig's truth, from *Zen and the Art of Motorcycle Maintenance*, that "The real cycle you're working on is the cycle called yourself."[1]

The afternoon after the "no-face" photo, Fiona and I biked to the south rim of Canyon de Chelly National Monument in Arizona. The sun was setting as we viewed the Spider Rock spire in an ancient canyon of caves where the Anasazi ("the forgotten ones") once dwelled. Returning to our motorcycle, we encountered two Navajo women selling jewelry and wood carvings. I approached one of them, encouraged by her curiosity about a tall white man looking dark-tanned and very road-tested. She claimed a certain wood carving was calling for me to purchase it.

*In Monument Valley in Utah, in front of a cliff-rock formation known as
the Ear of the Wind, John Quinlan unconsciously mirrors
the Vitruvian Man—and as "no-face," continues to shed his superficial self.*

I asked her why and she stared at me with wizened eyes. Still profoundly affected by the day before, I felt compelled to share my "no-face" experience with this native woman.

When I told her about the photo, her face contorted with alarm and fear. She warned me that this was not a good sign and reminded me that I *did* have a face; that I was ordained and blessed before I was born to be the wonderful and authentic self I was that day.

She assured me I was okay.

I smiled and reminded her that I *was* okay. More than okay. That I had now accepted this faceless anonymity. Inwardly, I smiled. My sense of freedom struck a chord. I did not have to know all of life's answers, nor did I need the credentials to know. I felt very natural and at ease; anonymous in an absolutely quiet, natural setting, stripped of my defining features. Surely, getting to the core of who we are should be this effortless! I was always taught that toil, struggle, control, and perfection were the red badges of courage. However, a quieter and more reflective path to the heart demands, possibly, a divergent type of courage—unrecognized and not glamorized—unprovoked and again open to being vulnerable.

I wondered what this revelation meant for me as an executive leadership coach. What purpose did the "no-face" experience fulfill? What were the applications for me and my executive coaching clients once I returned to Detroit? The "no-face" event turned out to be another evolvement in my personal development, resulting in a greater consciousness, gently encouraging me to embrace the self that has always been here, fully integrating with my true self—the good, the bad, and the ugly. To my amazement, I have realized that in order to find my true face, I have to lose the face that I present to the world. This takes loads of courage.

My "no-face" is my real face. Bad news for the aesthetic surgery industry.

I encourage my clients with the idea that sometimes you need to lose yourself in order to find yourself. Indeed, earlier on this particular trip, in the Delirium Wilderness of the Upper Peninsula, Michigan, I found myself on a dead-end gravel county road, surrounded by dense woods, lost and feeling quite vulnerable, yet I found my way back to where I made the wrong turn, and ultimately I got to my destination. I still prefer to motorcycle on "out of the way," quiet and scenic county roads. The reward of being vulnerable still outweighs the risk of getting lost.

My awareness of vulnerability that day in the desert emanated from a deep place within me. I knew then that the motorcycle trip had been worth the effort, providing me the opportunity to think about leadership in an enriched way. The spark had been lit.

I did purchase the carving.

When I returned home from the trip, my revelations about vulnerability and my true self that I'd gleaned from the "no-face" photo led directly to the book you now hold in your hands. I realized that at the core of change is vulnerability, but I also imagined a more empathetic manner of looking at leadership.

As I stared at the "no-face" photo in the weeks that followed, I realized that da Vinci's Vitruvian Man, which I'd unconsciously mirrored in the photo, perfectly matched the ten essential components that constituted my stalwart competitive leadership model of Alignment Strong. I knew this clear-cut vision linking Vitruvian Man to my leadership model would plainly illustrate the power of vulnerability and the strength of aligning an organization both from the top down and from the ground up. Then I began to think bigger. Based on all the positive feedback I'd received from thankful clients whose businesses began to see real results after my coaching, I knew I had to share this idea with a larger audience, including other leaders, coaches, teachers, and students. And so, the book *Alignment Strong* was born.

My business, financial, and economic background is ample, but I share this very personal story because I've realized in my vocation that it's the transformation of leaders themselves that is essential. *You* must become the change that you want evidenced in your organization. For optimal success, the integration of the strategic and human-centric systems will be the foundation on which you align the ten components of Alignment Strong. To become an effective leader, you must find deep integrity within yourself and embed this integrity in your organization. There must be a parallel developmental track and an intersect between personal and organizational change.

Subsequent to the motorcycle trip, my nephew David, a motorcycle aficionado, gave me, his outlier uncle, a book by Jack Kornfield titled *A Path with Heart*. Kornfield wrote, "The place where we can be most directly open to the mystery of life is in what we don't do well, in the places of our struggles and vulnerability. These places always require surrender and letting go. When we let ourselves become vulnerable, new things can be born in us. In risking the unknown we gain a sense of life itself."[2]

Does this mean that you have to hop on a motorcycle and head to the desert? Of course not. That's why I wrote *Alignment Strong* for you.

How You Can Use This Book

Some moments—some days—you're in the zone, executing tasks with pleasure and precision, empowering others with guidance they welcome, energizing your organization with harmony and vision.

On those days, you are aligned.

But did you plan to be?

By the end of this book, you will know how to align yourself and your business in an intentional way, and put the ten components of Alignment Strong into daily practice.

Such a sustained alignment can be brought to life systematically in a person, a company, or other kinds of organizations. Culturally strong-aligned companies financially outperform their misaligned competitors.

What form does this strong alignment take? Here's where da Vinci comes in—the Renaissance genius who outperformed his gifted competitors in a multiplicity of endeavors (which is, of course, your goal as a business leader). Da Vinci's Vitruvian Man, representing the ideal human form, is depicted at the end of this introduction.

The image of da Vinci's Vitruvian Man is universally recognized as the human form in perfect balance. While his drawing depicts the male figure, it categorically applies equally to women. The balance is about the form of the being, *not* the gender. The Vitruvian Man displays the underlying balance of the human being in the universe. Perhaps if da Vinci had been a woman, the drawing would be of the female form, and we would now know the iconic representation as the Vitruvian Woman. Regardless, I have always viewed Vitruvian Man as embodying the superlative *human* form, not the ideal *male* form, and find that this drawing represents balance for us all.

On the Vitruvian Man illustration I have placed the ten components of Alignment Strong. Each of the ten components positioned on the schematic contains a distillation, refinement, and shared wisdom I have gained over my years of practice. Encompassed in this simple illustration is pragmatism, which you can grasp without enduring academic exhaustiveness. By maximizing this model, transformation is a real possibility, for both you and your enterprise.

There is a plethora of helpful and not so helpful organizational literature in the marketplace, covering leadership, team building, cultural assessment, values, strategy, mission, performance management, and rewards. The content is overwhelming. Yet something is missing: a stake in the sand; a reference point. More specifically, a coherent and pragmatic change strategy is needed: an integrated framework to bring it all together, enabling your organization to achieve Alignment Strong.

Most of us have heard the saying, "Eat the elephant one bite at a time," when dealing with a large task, goal, or project. (Before you begin writing letters to PETA, this is a common phrase used in business, and I am *not* advocating actual consumption of the endangered African elephant!)

Akin to biting into an elephant, taken individually, each of my ten helpful techniques may cause more harm than good. Myopically, individuals may think they have captured what the complete elephant is like as they take their bite. But that's not a full, collective picture. It has been said that "when we try to pick out anything by itself we find it hitched to everything in the universe." Alignment Strong shows what the complete and aligned organization will look like. All the pieces come together.

Rest assured, I am not purporting a one-best-way, moving myself to a defensive posture. I have no need to enter into academic and professional discourse, possibly leading to exhaustive theoretical and semantic debate. I much prefer a good conversation, during which we can share our experiences and different perspectives; when we can learn from each other as practitioners. There are subject experts galore specializing in each component of Alignment Strong who can far outthink this practitioner. Yet I remind myself that the synthesis of knowledge and personal experience in this book would be difficult to replicate.

Alignment Strong is an organization-wide change process, offering a rational, holistic, road-tested framework that will help you keep all ten components in unison as you attend to your day job. In the chapters that follow, we will take a closer look at the Da Vinci Organizational Code, how you can embrace this method and utilize all of the ten components to your best advantage.

Now, the Vitruvian Man is da Vinci's study of the ideal proportions of the human form, perfected through fundamental mathematical applications. To me, Vitruvian Man also symbolizes the essential attributes that an integrated, culture-strong organization must possess: rationalistic thinking and problem solving, pragmatic action/execution, humanistic virtues/intentions, and artistry (leadership), all of which expresses the synthesis of Alignment Strong components, positioning the organization for health and sustainable competitive advantage.

This version of the Vitruvian Man strives toward perfect balance. I've spent a significant portion of my professional life seeking this balance in organizations, as an owner and a practitioner. This path led me to create a codification for a competitive leadership posture. Combining my thoughts with the Vitruvian Man, I created what I call the Da Vinci Organizational Code, which comprises all of the components of my Alignment Strong model shared with you in Chapters 1 through 3. This model will transform your role and the way your company operates. The case study in Chapter 4 assists in applying the code.

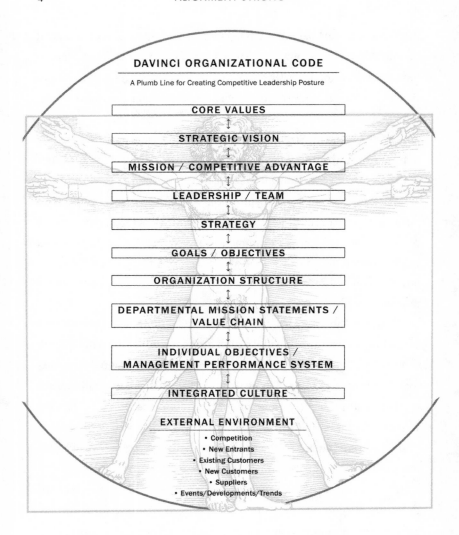

DAVINCI ORGANIZATIONAL CODE

A Plumb Line for Creating Competitive Leadership Posture

CORE VALUES

$\updownarrow$

STRATEGIC VISION

$\updownarrow$

MISSION / COMPETITIVE ADVANTAGE

$\updownarrow$

LEADERSHIP / TEAM

$\updownarrow$

STRATEGY

$\updownarrow$

GOALS / OBJECTIVES

$\updownarrow$

ORGANIZATION STRUCTURE

$\updownarrow$

DEPARTMENTAL MISSION STATEMENTS / VALUE CHAIN

$\updownarrow$

INDIVIDUAL OBJECTIVES / MANAGEMENT PERFORMANCE SYSTEM

$\updownarrow$

INTEGRATED CULTURE

EXTERNAL ENVIRONMENT

- Competition
- New Entrants
- Existing Customers
- New Customers
- Suppliers
- Events/Developments/Trends

All in balance: essential components for competitive leadership
as expressed with da Vinci's human ideal

Chapter 5, "Building Effective Relationships," is the entry into a deeper discourse on becoming more human-centric, beginning with yourself and including critical relationships.

This book comprises existential discourse, visceral experiences, rationalistic thinking, pragmatic actions, and raw emotion. You will discover fresh and lasting value throughout the text. Some of what you are reading here is built on and influenced by previous work by other authors. Without their contributions, I know Chapter 6, "Symphony of the Synthesist," would not have attained its dimensionality. The three subsections of this chapter are primed with experience, knowledge, reflection, and shared wisdom. I also created the Wisdom Life Chart to help you along on your developmental journey.

This is the way knowledge grows and is shared. And is inspired further.

Chapter 7, "The Internal Change Agent/The Aspiring Leader," wasn't much more than an afterthought until I dove deeper with the help of Kimberley Barker and other experts, and framed my own experiences, thoughts, and feelings about this subject. That effort turned out to be a real stretch for me, inviting me into greater vulnerability and originality. In particular, I hope this portion resonates with you.

"Final Thoughts" is carefully written to convey more meaning and tenor with fewer words. The Australian novelist Debra Adelaide wrote, "When writers get it right, it makes the result seem fluid and effortless, as if the story is warm honey the author has poured out in a single act, but also makes us feel the work is written for us alone."[1]

I have attempted to give credit where it is due, and in particular, the section titled "Wisdom's Invitation" specifies an entire library of sources that helped shape this book along with my own decades of relevant experience. Soon, perhaps, you may write a book, article, or slide show that happens to include something that leapt from here to your own consciousness. Or perhaps you're the author of something I have insufficiently recognized or even misunderstood. Let me know; in the next edition I will make amends.

As an author, I know that there are obvious distinctions between nonfiction and fiction, and as an executive coach, between the rational business and the personal human-centric as well. Yet there are similarities too. *Alignment Strong* may not be viewed as "warm honey poured out as a single act," but I do believe it attempts to bridge these confines in a personal and engaging manner.

Additionally, the Appendix provides self-directed assessments and management techniques to assist your organization's competitive leadership posture. Using research and support from the world's top thought leaders, authors, and business trailblazers, I've presented the established, effectual principles of Alignment Strong to turn your organization into a productive one that is humanistic, pragmatic, innovative, and poised to contend in the global marketplace.

Perhaps most important, you must realize that as a leader, you are the seen and unseen hero. I can provide practical knowledge and wisdom, but it is the leader who must emotionally commit wholeheartedly, find deep integrity within, and exemplify these essential elements to his or her organization. You, as the courageous leader, will use the lessons that follow from your experiences to align and transform your organization . . . and yourself. I have learned it is not what the vision is, but what the vision does.

Becoming Alignment Strong

Alignment Strong is a planned, organization-wide, and long-range change initiative; a leadership blueprint supported and affirmed from the top. It strategically improves an organization's problem-solving processes, efficiency, health, and competitive posture through the formulation/formation and linkage of **ten integral processes, practices, and systems** identified in the Vitruvian alignment schematic. The codification of these ten explicit components comprises the Da Vinci Organizational Code, which enables an organization to become and remain centered, strong, and competitively postured.

THE DA VINCI ORGANIZATIONAL CODE

Two statements by da Vinci himself dramatize this strongly aligned, organizational code:

- "People of accomplishment rarely sat back and let things happen to them. They went out and happened to things."
- "Realize that everything connects to everything else."

The Da Vinci Organizational Code is a series of ten components, exemplifying the emergence of leadership within an organizational system, adapting to the realities of the external environment. The ten components are sequenced as follows:

- **Core Values**
- **Strategic Vision**
- **Mission/Competitive Advantage**
- **Leadership/Team**
- **Strategy**
- **Goals/Objectives**
- **Organization Structure**
- **Departmental Mission Statements/Value Chain**
- **Individual Objectives/Management Performance System**
- **Integrated Culture**

I have observed, in thirty years of organization development practice, that there is a logical and natural design to Alignment Strong. Yet, as a third-party change agent, I have intervened at different landmarks. The purported alignment sequence may be rearranged, but having it supported and affirmed from the top is ideal, if not essential. Nevertheless, Alignment Strong participants will perceive, begin to comprehend, and welcome both an emergent/organic and deliberate/rationalistic ebb and flow.

The Da Vinci Organizational Code I've created has nothing to do with a secret society (that's a different book). Instead, it's about applying the harmony, strength, flexibility, and sheer humanity that the Vitruvian Man schematic illustrates. I interpret it as a code for competitive leadership posture that can and should be sustained throughout an organization, while being fully aware of the ecosystem to which it must adapt.

Adjusting this alignment is the plumb line, which is defined as a vertical line directed exactly toward the earth's center of gravity (according to the *American Heritage Science Dictionary*). Applied to the human body, the plumb line, symbolized by da Vinci's vertical marking down the middle of his Vitruvian Man, mathematically results in perfect alignment and balance. In business, an accurate plumb line results in a healthy and economically fit organization that is environmentally adaptive and regenerative. Within the Da Vinci Organizational Code, a plumb line assures competitive leadership posture.

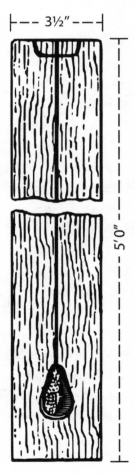

Plumb Line Clarity

Let me dispel any unfamiliarity you may have with the term *plumb line*. You are not alone. The PhD organization development practitioner and university instructor who critically reviewed my manuscript before publication was unaware of the term. So were all three of my college-degree daughters. Maybe that's the problem. They all have college degrees; a plumb line originated as a tool for construction, not in the classroom. Use of the instrument is traced back to the building of the Egyptian pyramids and is mentioned in the Old Testament.

One of my previous clients, Perry Merlo, president of Merlo Construction Company, shared with me that he was introduced to a plumb line at the age of nine by his dad, Reno Joseph Merlo, who founded the company in 1946. It's a vertical measuring tool consisting of a string with a teardrop-shaped weight attached (a plumb bob). This simple tool is used to

The plumb line—a simple string attached to a plumb bob (weight) used around the time of the building of the pyramids—determines true alignment.

measure the verticality of walls, forms, and columns, to set anchor bolts, to apply wallpaper, and to pour cement, all with precise accuracy. Also, a plumb line centers highway survey telescopes called transit levels. Today, the highway crews you see in the orange jackets and plastic helmets use optical plummets instead of plumb bobs to position their transit levels along the correct lines.

Without plumb lines, things end up jagged, uneven, crooked, and awry, including highways. Alignment is critical.

How do you measure alignment in an organization?

Research by Denison Consulting shows how one can measure culture in a way that is useful to organizations because it links culture with other bottom-line performance measures. Their scrutiny affirms the Alignment Strong competitive leadership model. Culturally strong-aligned companies financially outperform their misaligned competitors. Denison's research concludes that "culture has not only short-term impact on performance but lasting effects as a competitive edge. Specifically, this research has shown an advantage on ROA, sales growth, and market value for organizations scoring in the top 25% (vs. bottom) on the Denison Organization Culture Survey (DOCS)."[1] Accordingly, by adopting Alignment Strong's ten components, financial expectations for market share expansion and enhanced profitability are more accurate and competitive, even taking into account the headwinds of the external environment.

Let's look again at Leonardo da Vinci's Vitruvian Man in order to see how the ideal alignment of the human form mirrors the perfect alignment of your organization. You will also realize how this plumb line as applied to da Vinci's Vitruvian Man represents unrivaled alignment within your company.

ALIGNMENT IDEAL

Da Vinci's Vitruvian Man portrays perfect posture alignment. This ideal state of homeostasis causes the least amount of musculoskeletal pain and strain. Most of us have experienced lower back pain, strained muscles, dislocations, and sore joints. For your organization, these tedious pains may be translated as a lack of accountability, customer attrition, quality failures, stale culture, high turnover, and/or lackluster financial performance.

By using the Da Vinci Organizational Code—the conscious and consistent alignment of the schematic's ten components—your organization will achieve greater ease and fluidity. Posture experts describe ideal alignment in terms of the locations of body parts used as landmarks, relative to the vertical **plumb line** that runs down your center. A similar plumb line within your own organization connects the opposite ends of the axis, top to bottom. The Alignment Strong leadership model assists an organization in aligning its "ten body parts," or landmarks, to their imagined plumb line, enabling it to establish homeostasis with the external environment. In such a posture, the organization is prepared to embrace the task/demands (e.g., product innovation, competitive pricing, extraordinary customer service) of the external environment while optimizing strength and maintaining balance.

MISALIGNMENT LEGACY

The Alignment Strong leadership model requires astuteness. Without this wisdom, organizational breakdowns can occur right at the beginning or at the top of the schematic, where core values, strategic vision, and mission were formulated and articulated haphazardly. This shows that the credibility of the CEO and leadership team has been diminished. Predictably, strategy execution is then problematic; supporting goals at the middle to lower levels are not truly aligned to authentic and accurate expectations. These issues result when an organization becomes misaligned.

Consequently, operational excellence initiatives languish. Morale is impacted. Employees mentally and emotionally disengage. Turnover increases, adding to recruitment, training, and retention costs. The disruptive loss of critical employees undercuts the P&L, putting additional pressure on short-term/tactical objectives at the expense of long-term strategic goals. Consistent research confirms that most CEOs today face this dilemma of balancing long-term and short-term goals.

Misalignment, as defined by *Webster's New World Dictionary*, is "the incorrect positioning or placement of something." The juxtaposition— alignment—is "the process of adjusting parts so that they are in a proper relative position." Clearly, the goal of a leader is to bring his or her organization into total and complete alignment.

But how do you get there?

I will show you.

ALIGNMENT FRAMEWORK

This book provides a framework—like the Vitruvian bones, ligaments, and muscles—for sorting out your experiences, and prioritizing your acquired knowledge toward organizational progress and personal development. Continual feedback and evaluation for the organization and leader underscores agile learning.

Using the Da Vinci Organizational Code, you will find your own strong alignment, complete with a plumb line of perfect balance, enabling you to adapt continually and stay buoyant amid an ever-changing external environment. You will see how things line up and how modularity reduces complexity. You will see sequential patterns. You will see interdependence. You will see how sets of patterns can mesh. You will gain strong alignment in order to be Alignment Strong.

From that position, you can regard any particular organizational process—from its founding or birthing through ultimate consequences—and look both back, in evaluation, and forward, in prediction. You can know why things are a certain way. Your wisdom will be built on quality, a summation of your experiences, and garnered knowledge.

You will care differently about things and you will know why. You will store energy through discernment, the wisdom gatekeeper. You will gain clarity and resolve through emotional commitments.

You *and* your organization will become aligned strongly.

Embracing Change

A lignment Strong is akin to a developmental journey. And this entire developmental journey is based on change, which is subtle and complex. A change process is usually incremental, as contrasted to revolutionary. Parallel change initiatives may coexist as well. Leaders begin to manifest a sixth sense as they recognize the need for change. They become more knowledgeable as to where there is ripeness for change in the interior landscape of their own organization (e.g., leadership, team development, mission clarity, core values, strategic vision) or where the external impetus (e.g., threat of competition, suppliers, customers, economic cycles, political-social trends) may be identified in the **external environment**, shown at the bottom of the Da Vinci Organizational Code schematic.

The optimal **fit/match** of the organization to the external operating environment and of individuals to the enterprise's goals is a never-ending, unscripted search for congruency. Change is not managed. To the contrary, the aim is to create your own container or petri dish to let change germinate. The right conditions need to be set for sprouts to take root.

Let's talk a little more about change. After losing my publicly traded company, I returned to a university to obtain a master of science degree in organization development (MSOD). One of the first questions posed to us students (most of us out of undergraduate school for at least ten years) was, "What is your theory for change?"

That's a valid question for anyone running a company in the ever-increasing flux of today's world. That day I began to formulate my own theory of change, which became foundational for my personal growth and consulting as an executive coach over the next thirty years.

So what is *your* theory for change? Let me assist you by sharing my own path of discovery full of surprises, juxtapositions, and questions.

At times, to my chagrin and resignation, Lord Tennyson's mandate "Change is the great certainty" became my baseline tenet pertaining to transformational change. It was my starting point and, admittedly, with occasional adjournments and abjections, rings true to this day. From a literary perspective, I emotionally connected to many writers throughout the years. For instance, in a state of futility and humor, the author Thomas McGuane, in his novel *Ninety-Two in the Shade*, admitted, "I consider the wonder of the things that befall me, convinced that my life was the best omelet you can make with a chainsaw."[1] Now, let's be honest, haven't all of us felt this way, at one time or another? Also, personally and spiritually, I have been counseled and mentored to embrace change.

The corn parable espoused by Jesus Christ, that a seed must fall into the ground and die in order to bring forth fruit, and the Buddha koan "whatever we practice we become" evoke an eagerness to learn. They encourage and give me hope that a "beginner's mind" may be a good starting point. Plato, philosopher and author of the ancient dialogue *Phaedrus*, mused with his audience, including me, by wistfully exclaiming, "May your inner and outer man become one." Robert Pirsig also leveraged off Plato in his critically acclaimed treatise on values, *Zen and the Art of Motorcycle Maintenance*. As a biker for over fifty years, I've also concluded, as Pirsig did, that "the real cycle you're working on is the cycle called yourself."

The poems of the thirteenth-century Persian and Sufi mystic Rumi were also encouraging to me as I formulated my own theory on change. Rumi's writings conveyed to me that inward change and knowledge "is a fountainhead from within you, moving out . . . [a] tablet, one already completed and preserved inside you. A spring overflowing its springbox. A freshness in the center of the chest . . . It's fluid, and it doesn't move from outside to inside through the conduits of plumbing–learning."[2]

What these thinkers realized, and I've determined as well, is there is deeper meaning and purpose to change. There is an endgame, both for oneself and one's organization. As cited by the adult learning theorist Robert Kegan, and explained by authors Jennifer Garvey Berger and Catherine Fitzgerald in their text, *Executive Coaching: Practices & Perspectives*, "Transformation occurs when we develop the ability to step back and reflect on something that used to be hidden or taken for granted and then make decisions about it. That transformational learning happens when someone changes not just the way he behaves, not just the way he feels, but the way he knows—not just what he knows but the way he knows."[3]

I was grounded by behavioral science and personality theory in order to receive my graduate degree, and I've always been interested in these subjects in relation to leadership. The psychologist Alfred Adler said, "Our behavior is determined by our perception of what we hope to achieve in the future, not what we have done . . . or what has been done to us in the past."[4] Over the years, I have also gradually discovered that most individuals committed to personal growth realize there is a decrease or contraction in their own egocentricity. Usually humility and vulnerability are evidenced, which are attributes of servant leadership. Thought leaders Jim Collins, Ken Wilber, and Brené Brown gave me a helping hand by sharing their perspectives on one's ego.

In a business context, former General Electric CEO Jack Welch and business author Noel M. Tichy exclaimed with deliberation, "Control your destiny or someone else will." Competitively appealing and forceful as this may resonate, can it be that simple? Bruce Gibb, an organizational psychologist and a practitioner for five decades, reminded me that the burning conviction to take control of your organizational destiny may end up being counterproductive to building trust, teamwork, and individual confidence. Indeed, change is far more comprehensive and subtler than I first realized. One's passion may work against one's best intentions. Be careful about the words, statements, and initiatives you unleash in your enterprise; they may undermine your best intentions.

"Do or die" is another battle cry put forth by strategy experts, leveraging off the fearful consequences of doing nothing as opposed to calculated risk-taking. I appreciate the sense of urgency these mantras express. John P. Kotter, in his book *Leading Change,* explains that this emotional conviction, "a sense of urgency," is an essential element for forceful change.[5]

PricewaterhouseCoopers annually publishes business survey results, inevitably concluding that CEOs continue to struggle at balancing long-term and short-term priorities. Indeed, change is hard, especially at the top. Usually, long-term visioning/strategizing and sustained change efforts get the short end of the stick. Predictably, when push comes to shove, the intuitive, more organic, and emergent attributes of long-term vision and strategy are toned down to meet short-term planning priorities, propagating an organization-wide, risk-averse, and fixed mindset. A more integrated approach is needed. This necessitates the willingness to become competent in both activities, as different and conflicting as they may be. Sir John Whitmore, author of *Coaching for Performance* (especially the last chapter on advanced coaching), as well as Carol S. Dweck, who wrote *Mindset*, were essential reads for me to comprehend that such contradictions need to be fused in order for the leader to be effective. It takes courage and stamina to stay this course.

The strategy author Roger Martin highlights the closed-thinking, certainty-bound, anti-volatility strategy mindset, propagated by members of the C-suite, particularly regarding an organization's financial function. By limiting strategic choice, a change resistance permeates the organization's goal setting, reinforcing an aversion to long-term planning and risk.

In the *Harvard Business Review* article "The Big Lie of Strategic Planning," Martin comments, "Mistaking planning for strategy is a common trap. Even board members, who are supposed to be keeping managers honest about strategy, fall into it. They are, after all, primarily current or former managers, who find it safer to supervise planning than to encourage strategic choice. Moreover, Wall Street is more interested in the short-term goals described in plans than in the long-term goals that are the focus of strategy. Analysts pore over plans in order to assess whether companies can meet their quarterly goals."[6]

Yet there may be hope for even change-resistant, certainty-bound Wall Street. Are they slightly beginning to incorporate the *Built to Last* paradigm (popularized by the author Jim Collins, who also wrote the best seller *Good to Great*) into their buy-sell-hold investment analyses? Is Wall Street taking a longer and more strategic view of the importance of companies authentically committing, budgeting, and developing human capital? Hold on there. Is this suggesting people are worth the capital investment?

Edgar Schein, professor emeritus at the MIT Sloan School of Management, penned a book titled *Helping* and authored, years later, the publication *Humble Leadership*. Provoked and touched by his thoughts, within a change framework, I inquired, "Is there a link to/with strategy, economic goals, social goals, and cultural values? If there is, what is it? Why is it integral to change?" After decades in the field, Schein cut to the chase and deduced that authentic, personalized, and effective interpersonal, group, and organizational relationships are the guardrails for transformational change. He clarifies, "this is a reciprocal process between two parties that must be or at least be seen to be fair and equitable."[7] He further imparts that this reciprocal process is a social economic exchange and is a universal communication method that engenders trust.

Take a moment and ask if all three of my preceding questions have been answered. Trust is the cornerstone/keystone for planned change.

A few years ago, at Google world headquarters, Schein, as the keynote speaker, led a discussion on leadership. I viewed it on YouTube. What a treat. His audience was made up of young, aspiring Google members. The C-suite, outside of the representative, host, and facilitator, was visibly absent or never introduced. Schein concluded his globally wired interactive talk on the subject of authentic workplace relationships and real-time personal interactions with vigor by candidly asserting that relationships do count; otherwise, one is plain stupid. Bursting with laughter, I clapped my hands.

Lately, I heard that the senescent Wall Street mantra of "greed is good" had been displaced by an advanced mantra that "purpose is good." However, seeing is believing. But never say never. Icebergs do melt.

In 2008, while motorcycling to the east entrance of Glacier National Park in Montana, I pulled into a tavern and passed an old pickup truck parked in the lot. As I made my way inside, a yelping dog in the truck bed almost distracted me from noticing a rusted signature plate in the back window, next to the gun rack. I took a closer look at the inscription and recognized a quote from the Greek philosopher Heraclitus of Ephesus (535 BC–475 BC): "Change is the only constant." I cannot think of another.

Enough rumination. Let me share with you a tested change formula.

THE CHANGE FORMULA

As a change consultant, I assist CEOs in sorting out long-term and short-term priorities and timelines. Invariably, a change strategy is discussed, framed, and adopted. I impart a simple yet powerful formula that Bruce Gibb shared with me, which was created by then–management consultant David Gleicher, simplified by Kathleen Dannemiller, and slightly modified and interpreted by myself. Kathie was the sponsor for my MSOD degree at American University in Washington, DC, and became a mentor and friend.

The change formula helps the CEO to comprehend the motivational factors/variables not captured in a spreadsheet, strategy narrative, or introductory executive summary of an annual strategic plan.

The change framework formula: $C = D \times V \times F > R$

C = Change (transformation: to replace one thing with another)

D = Dissatisfaction (discomfort, pain, crisis) with the current state/present

V = Vision (target for the future; what is preferred as opposed to predicted)

F = First steps (the plan, with deliberate/cognitive actions to realize the vision)

R = Resistance to change (obstacles, restraints, personal and organizational defensive routines)

Multiplying the three variables $D \times V \times F$ creates the critical mass and momentum greater than (>) the resistance (R) to change, propelling the organization to a new state or level of change (C). The art form is to utilize the variables (levers) deftly and with integrity. When and how to use those variables takes practice; watching the results when others try it is instructive. A leader must also incorporate external factors, such as industry, economic, political, and social trends; competitor and supplier analysis; and customer expectations to combat insular thinking.

For over three decades, I have found most CEOs and organizations are nudged or forced to change because of dissatisfaction (D). Also, I have learned that for a CEO to overcome personal and organizational resistance to change (R), he or she has to be willing to move out of invulnerability and a fixed mindset and into vulnerability and a growth mindset.

Self-examination into one's personal change resistance is warranted. What you personally resist and why you resist it may significantly influence strategic vision, competitive posture, and business strategy. In a position of power, personal and strategic blind spots frequently play off of and reinforce one another to the peril of the enterprise. I have witnessed vision (**V**) distortions (e.g., grandiose risk-taking, unimpressive risk aversion) emanating from intractable defensive postures related to personal change resistance from CEOs. It often felt and looked like their lives depended on it. Carl Jung cautioned, "What you resist not only persists, but will grow in size." Leon F. Seltzer, pivoting off Jung in a *Psychology Today* article titled "You Only Get More of What You Resist —Why?" suggests acceptance of what is, or what isn't (e.g., brutal facts), so you can move on.[8]

Openness to change (**C**) expedites them in becoming an agent of effective change, a co-learner—open to ideas and feedback—owning mistakes and creating psychologically safe dialogues for betterment. Such behaviors begin to erode defensive routines and dilute the fear of failure.

I have further concluded that a strong bias to forward-prospective thinking captured in a compelling vision (**V**) is a vital antidote to the resistance (**R**) to change. Without the emotional intelligence and competence of inspirational leadership (e.g., guiding and motivating with a compelling vision), as author Daniel Goleman defines, the variable titled vision (**V**) is diluted, fortifying the resistance (**R**) to change.

Many CEOs attempt first steps (**F**) and short-term fixes, but these initiatives often die out and usually go to the flavor-of-the-month graveyard. Some companies are galvanized by a strategic vision (**V**) yet have not fully integrated dissatisfaction (**D**) and first steps (**F**).

When I was living my former life as a rainforest coffee entrepreneur, I was initially invited up to the remote Managalas Plateau of Oro Province, Papua New Guinea, where the farmers were burning their coffee beans, protesting exorbitantly low or no payments received for their work. They demonstrated this not only with fire but also through a staged drama during which the women were weeping for their husbands. So began my seven-year foray to help those 2,300 farmers by building a company. Their initial dissatisfaction (**D**) brought them much pain. Integrating vision (**V**) and first steps (**F**) led them to changes (**C**), resulting in extraordinary increases of farm-gate prices for their coffee beans, besides creating brand awareness in the global marketplace. Ultimately, the inertia (loss of hope), obstacles (no vehicles and pulping machines), and restraints (corrupt politicians and terrible roads) creating this Gordian knot—labeled resistance (**R**)—were overcome.

What variable today is the driving force to propel change for you? What variable moves your organization off the status quo? What would be the sequence of the variables for effective change to take place for you and your organization?

Take some time to think through your answers. Jot them down and then predict what the responses would be for your executive team before you solicit their input. How accurate will you be? What is the formula for change for yourself and for your company today? Such a process may expose your own personal and organizational blind spots.

Remember, transformational change is largely imperceptible when you are in it. Ask any caterpillar. A change theory could be the guide you need to the future and be a light on your path of discovery for yourself and your organization.

THE STRUGGLE FOR CHANGE

CEOs often sense the need for change, and they perhaps act to deal with one symptom or another of them, singly. That's like strengthening the biceps while allowing the wrists to lack flexibility or the feet to continue plodding. What's needed is a full-circle-plus-plumb-line framework that enables change to take hold and becomes self-evolving.

As internal change agents, leaders acquire the competencies of self and social awareness. Reflection is demanded. A serious time commitment is required in order to slow down to comprehend each step and where it fits in. It is ironic. On the horizon, a flywheel kicks in, and things seem to speed up. So fast, your organization may be faced with other challenges called controlled growth. The demand for your products and services can exceed your supply (capabilities and capacities) within your organization's internal value chain.

But importantly, Alignment Strong is not a one-time, short-term remedy. From the start, its newly minted organizational design will always be open to revision. It is contingent to the demand tasks of the external environment. Leadership's ego, which has far-reaching tentacles to influence the mindset of the culture, should be dispassionate about personal strengths and limitations. To be relevant, the C-suite's role definitions need to be grounded by accurate self-assessment and open to revision.

Elaborating on accurate self-assessment, I always communicate to a potential client—a CEO to be coached—that we do an initial intake. One coach describes this as a "filtration process" to determine if there is a good fit. During this sensing phase, together we examine the potentiality of the relationship. This process focuses specifically on a prospect's struggles much more than on his or her goals, dreams, and visions, because in most cases the struggles give a much more informative and accurate picture of what the main need is for coaching/consulting. Recently, early on in our relationship, the president of a manufacturing company disclosed, "I will be vulnerable with you, John. I must be vulnerable with myself, willing to look at myself, in order for this to work." Korn Ferry, the executive search retention and training firm, described the optimal "coachee": "This candidate has a growing awareness of the need for change, underscored by an intrinsic need to grow, and is a lifelong learner. This person has a realistic sense of self, accepts feedback, and shows an earnest desire to improve."[9]

Somerset Maugham's iconic novel *The Razor's Edge* appropriately names the uncomfortable place one must travel to go against the grain, but that is where the growth is to be found. It is a conscious, determined, and courageous effort to attain quality leadership.

In my experience, goals are easier to achieve when you address the causes of the struggles. An executive coach, whose name escapes me, shared that clients are usually very clear and conscious of their struggles, but very fuzzy around their goals. My initial inquiry of a client may revolve around his or her interior roadblocks: patterns of behavior, defensive routines, or deeply held assumptions and beliefs that continue to undermine and subvert one's best intentions. Three questions I ask are: What do you do when you're really up against it? What can I say to you when you are most stuck—dealing with your "struggles"—that will return you to action? What makes you think I may be able to help you accomplish this?

This means that if we move forward to an engagement (we may not if the answers are too flimsy), I have a good level of understanding of my client's struggles, that they are the kind of thoughtful and self-examining person that I prefer to work with, that they make the effort and will take the time to think through responses and communicate them with me (and not deflect or obscure their answers), and very importantly, it means that I can approach the relationship as a committed helper versus a consultant marketing myself in need of fees, income, and acclaim. I've assembled a few questions that you should ask in regard to what is really motivating you to continue reading.

1. Why are you reading this book? Why are you seeking leadership advice?
2. Why did you purchase this book? What are you hoping this book can help you with?
3. What is making it difficult to accomplish these things alone?

4. What have you tried already in relation to this? What other books/texts have you read?

5. How successful have each of these approaches been? Have the other books/texts helped you?

6. Why do you think you still have not accomplished your goals? What worked or didn't work with other books?

7. How do you think this book may help you accomplish your goals?

8. Already, what has drawn you into this book that makes you feel this book is written for you alone?

On a deeper level, ask these questions of yourself in the framework of why you are seeking change within yourself as a leader or within your organization. You may uncover the answers you need to move forward and find fundamental, necessary growth.

Now, we are going to shift the conversation from the "struggle for change" to another discussion, to make sure we're clear on the terminology and fundamental ideas of Alignment Strong moving forward. Let's check the fundamentals.

ALIGNMENT STRONG'S CHANGE TERMS AND NOMENCLATURE

Organization Development (OD): A planned, organization-wide, and long-range change initiative, supported and affirmed from the top. It strategically improves an organization's problem-solving processes, effectiveness, efficiency, health, and competitive posture, through planned interventions in the organizational processes, using behavioral science knowledge. The assistance of an external change agent, or third party, and the use of the theory and technology of applied behavioral science are required.

Accordingly, Alignment Strong is grafted into the traditional field of the science of organization development, founded by Kurt Lewin and other trailblazers, including (to name a few) Gordon and Larry Lippitt, Wendell French and Cecil Bell, Chris Argyris, Warren Bennis, Richard Beckhard, Marvin Weisbord, Frank Friedlander, Robert Tannenbaum, Charlie and Edith Seashore, Edgar Schein, Peter Vaill, and Robert Marshak. The preceding definition/description is a blend of their understandings. As a result, Alignment Strong is eclectic and inextricably tied to this field. Organization development should not be confused, misconstrued, or quickly labeled as solely an adjunct of HR, leadership, team building, cultural assessment, or training initiatives. To the contrary, it integrates all of these distinct and valuable roles and efforts into a meta framework. Today, this may be a different-than-usual way of thinking about the topic. For the uninitiated, it can lead into uncharted but fertile waters. Noteworthy: the OD field is the original purveyor of a unified organizational change theory.

Integral Processes–Practices–Systems: Tried and tested concepts, theories, and methodologies, consistently applied, are necessary to make the whole complete, in order to establish organizational alignment. These are the detailed components of Alignment Strong.

Action Research Method: The transformation process of continually diagnosing, researching, and assessing the *current state*, to develop change premises and forward actions, in order to move the organization to its preferred *target*. This continuous reflection learning process is embedded into the organization's mindset and culture, assuring forward movement. It is evidenced by a *plan* supported by specific objectives to reduce the gap between the current state and the preferred target. Evaluation and reflection always follow.

STP Model: A gap analysis schematic, utilized in strategic planning, representing State–Target–Plan variables, emblematic of the emergent learning nature of action research. The three variables of the triangle are of equal significance. The distortion/modification of any one of the variables will amplify or diminish the trajectory of the organization. The gap between the state and target produces an energy called creative tension, which is channeled into an effective plan and supported by empowered members.

Contingency Approach: There is no one best way to organize and control the planning of an organization. There are no universal solutions (single best way) to manage or solve problems. It is a consistent search for appropriate processes and practices to find methods of solution and management for different situations and conditions, both internally and externally.

External Environment: The setting or conditions where an organization operates:

- Existing customers, new customers, competition, new entrants, and suppliers
- Events, developments, and trends in your industry
- Political, economic, social, technological, and legal threats and/or opportunities

Internal and External Fit: The fit/match-up of organizational capability/capacity to the task demands of the external environment as well as the fit/match-up between individual needs and organizational goals, which impact the optimization of social and technical resources. The elimination of gaps and dissonance on these two dimensions creates congruency resulting in greater organization and individual performance.

Homeostasis: The tendency toward a relatively stable equilibrium among interdependent elements, such as the internal organization and its surroundings. Homeostasis is maintained by feedback loops (like a thermostat in a house). A 360-degree assessment on C-suite leadership effectiveness is an internal feedback loop, contrasted to external customer feedback, assessing one's products and services.

TARGET

Strategic Vision

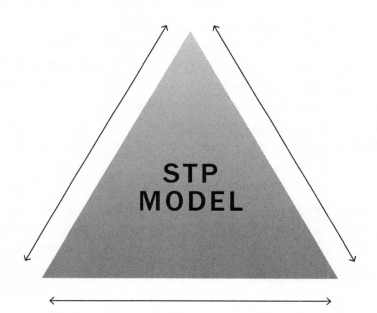

STP
MODEL

STATE (CURRENT)   # PLAN

- Internal Strengths
- Internal Weaknesses
- External Opportunities
- External Threats

- Strategy
- Goals
- Objectives

The three variables—the points of the triangle—are always in dynamic tension.
This gap analysis tool is a fundamental habit the CEO should acquire
to consistently view his or her organization.

Socio-technical System/Open System: The "whole" system framework of transforming inputs into outputs, whereby the inputs of capital, time, assets, and knowledge are transformed by the throughput process (value chain) into the outputs of delivered products and services. The integration of the socio (human) system and technical system is the glue and lubricant of the organization's internal value chain. Also, it may be called your "secret culture sauce," differentiating you from your rivals. Operating in the external environment, the integrated/joint system—your own internal value chain—is open and speedily adjusts itself to the feedback it receives from customers, suppliers, and marketplace intelligence. In a nutshell, a whole-system framework led by the CEO is an effective method for accelerated change.

Value Chain: Traditionally, we have viewed organizations vertically, where a "command and control" view of the enterprise prevails. Surprisingly, this perspective is still embedded in many organizations today. Viewing the organization horizontally introduces a more expansive and collaborative framework, where defined and discreet departmental/functional outputs/deliverables are clearly viewed, exemplifying internal customer/vendor linkages and relationships. The value chain, uniquely understood and environmentally adaptive, will be postured to deliver one's value proposition: competitive advantage.

THE ENDGAME

With fundamental balance established, your organization can achieve adaptivity or buoyancy (homeostasis) in the external environment, assuring the organization's sustainability. This is Alignment Strong; this is the endgame to counteract organizational entropy leading to extinction. With this method, you will culturally embed an appetite for change within your organization. You and members of your team will understand that change and transformation are now ceaseless dynamics spiraling upward.

Now that we've explored the overarching framework of this leadership model, let's take a closer look at the ten components that will align and strengthen your organization.

The Ten Components of the Da Vinci Organizational Code

We can now look again, with deeper scrutiny, at Alignment Strong's Vitruvian Man and my translation of the Da Vinci Organizational Code. As I previously mentioned, there are ten components that make up this leadership code, providing strong alignment for an organization.

The ten components are as follows:

- **Core Values**
- **Strategic Vision**
- **Mission/Competitive Advantage**
- **Leadership/Team**
- **Strategy**
- **Goals/Objectives**
- **Organization Structure**
- **Departmental Mission Statements/Value Chain**
- **Individual Objectives/Management Performance System**
- **Integrated Culture**

Each of the ten components is integral to complete the code. Now, let's get down to business.

1. CORE VALUES

These are an organization's deeply held and uncompromising beliefs, including assumptions. Core values are the *raison d'être* and purpose of the organization. Shared values are espoused, firstly, by leadership and are supported by norms (expected behaviors). Leadership author Simon Sinek deduced that it is not about *what* you do but *why* you do what you do. The mindset of the organization has been or will be spawned by its core values. The impact of these values—whether moral or immoral, healthy or unhealthy, well-intentioned or ill-intentioned—resonates, for better or worse, with employees internally, and externally with critical stakeholders (e.g., community, customers, and suppliers). Core values are the bedrock of the culture, the barometer of the organizational climate, the cornerstone of competitive advantage, and a company's brand identity. They support or impede movement toward the next component: strategic vision.

Make no mistake: living by stated corporate values is difficult. It takes courage to defend core values, especially during conflict with board and team members. Patrick Lencioni, president of The Table Group and a renowned speaker on leadership, wrote, "After all, it's much harder to be clear and unapologetic for what you stand for than to cave in to politically correct pressures."[1]

The development of a shared values statement, which details these core principles, demands a willingness by leadership to suspend personal assumptions and preferences in order to engage in dialogue with members of an organization. This is a chance to slow down for reflection and introspection; to gather together critical stakeholders (e.g., founders, shareholders) as well as the top of the organization to share perspectives and stories. Surprisingly, most organizations have not given much thought to the origin of their stated core values. Platitudes on the C-suite walls or lobby hallways, website citations, and one-off retreat agenda items are worthy attempts. In some cases, a social media or PR firm has been contracted to do the tedious work of wordsmithing. Yet these best intentions may be more meaningful than what is actually being communicated and displayed within the organization. Usually, these "surface" stated values are a hybrid of personal values—which may comprise those of the founders, board, CEO, and C-suite—including biases and organizational history (critical events and heroics), and aspirational-inspirational values that "feel good," yet have little substance. Let's continue to bore deeper to get to the bedrock.

A simple and non-exhaustive inquiry, during which a leader invites members to rank and share their personal values and beliefs, has been an eye-opener for many owners, family councils, and the C-suite. While there are loads of values assessments in the marketplace, the following exercise is a good beginning point for you and your organization to begin discovering its true core values. This practice opens up a multitude of personal perspectives.

The storytelling aspect of the exercise ("Where did this personal value or belief originate?") may be a remarkable and compelling experience, full of surprises, curiosity, intuition, and even clashes. The conversations will inevitably become more expansive. Personal visions will begin to percolate. Often, an individual will empathically state during the exercise, "Not only do I comprehend this value, but this is what I want to guide my life as well as our enterprise."

Presto! A line has been crossed. An ideal alignment has been manifested whereby personal values, personal visions, and organizational values are inextricably linked. Emotional commitment will predictably rise when these personal and organizational values synchronize. Logically, the next step is to formulate the strategic vision for the company, further clarifying the alignment of personal values, personal visions, organizational values, and the strategic vision.

Here is the valuable exercise for clarifying personal values. Ideally, you and your core team would do this simultaneously and then compare the results.

Personal Values Inquiry

Below are ten values/beliefs/principles (of course, these are different than the ten components of the code; I simply like to work in groups of ten). This exercise serves as a starting point, stimulating a conversation around comparative values. Reflect on each value that follows and then rank them in importance from 1 to 10, with 1 being the most important to you and 10 being the least important to you. Keep in mind, these are personal *and* organizational.

1 = Most important to you personally   10 = Least important to you personally

Professional image: _____
Your business reputation is critical

Influence: _____
Achievement of business goals (e.g., financial results)

Personal satisfaction: _____
Fun and excitement

Quality of life: _____
Leisure time for you and your family

Material wealth: _____
For pleasure and/or stature

Respect of peers: _____
To be authentically esteemed and trusted

Altruism: _____
Contribution to community/society/environment

Pleasing others: _____
Deep satisfaction in being helpful, appreciated, and in harmony with colleagues

Personal/developmental goals: _____
Learning, growth commitments, and opportunities are highly prized

Meaning and purpose: _____

The motivation or intrinsic reward that drives emotional commitment

(Note: Deal and Kennedy's *Corporate Cultures* inspired this exercise.[2])

An organization's leader will be able to perceive where personal and organizational values are not only linked, but potentially aimed. The leader will establish a true-north compass point for the organization. Without such a compass in place, the enterprise will have great difficulty reaching its destination and more than likely will not arrive with the original vision intact. But if the compass is constant, true-north readings (espousing the organization's values) will now be evidenced, for instance, in consistent product and service offerings, brand strategy, recruitment practices, onboarding process, performance management, compensation practices, sanctions, and terminations. All aspects of the organization will become infused with the established core values.

Over the years, a number of shared values have been identified and supported by investigating which norms or expected behaviors activate those values. I'll give you a sampling of the supporting norms and the resultant shared values from a recent client of mine.

A dominant shareholder and CEO, who did not start but purchased a company, huddled together with two senior executives/minority shareholders. They examined, developed, and shared their own life charts—their personal histories that trace where their own values and assumptions originated from (e.g., successes, failures, abuse/emotional deprivation, love/affirmation, tragedy, critical events, wounds, healthy and unhealthy influencers). As I reflect, their retrospection was both fluid and static. The participants began whenever and wherever they chose. Most of my clients, as they did, started on the playground and early school, with family or no family, a sporting feat or failure; usually somewhere in between the ages of ten and sixteen.

This owner/CEO and two executives penned, typed, drew, painted, and even cut and pasted magazine pictures. This process is intimate, whether the metaphor and medium are connected with sequential boxes or circles, represented by trails of valleys and mountains, a necklace, a totem pole, or concentric circles; whether one uses a spreadsheet, an upward and/or downward spiral, or a workflow schematic, the life charts are enhanced by colors, animals, and symbols. The configurations are revealing, full of meaning, and infinite.

Take a look at the handout that follows. It is part of a larger compendium on values I give to my coachees.

Life Chart Development/Analysis/Application

I: Identity	II: Pinpoint	III: Core Values	IV: Assumptions
• Events • Successes • Failures • Profound experiences	• What • When • Where	What life principles/values have evolved from I & II that presently characterize who you are today	What underlying value assumptions and associated behaviors need to be explored and reflected upon in order to become a more effective leader

Pick your medium (e.g., curves, graph, wave lengths, boxes, itemized statements), analogy, or metaphor to life chart out your past, going back as far as you can account. Mark each important event within your configuration of choice, and give yourself the freedom to let it take on any form: straight, curved, messy, precise. Take private time to "let it flow and emerge." If you wish, use different colors to distinguish time periods or events.

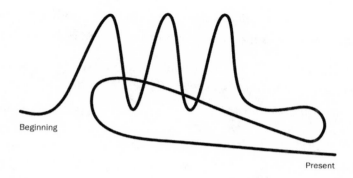

A life chart can show waves of ups and downs, and reversals.

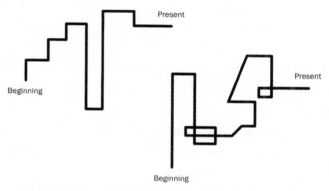

A life chart may show step-by-step progress, great leaps and falls,
backtracking, and progression.

These life charts helped my client discover where the cultural DNA of his present organization was, inspiring him to continue to shape and mold the mindset of the enterprise. The CEO and two colleagues examined, as per instruction, the enterprise's past values and current stated values. Their concoction was now ready for interpersonal discourse. Over three months, these three leaders created a new statement of core values that better epitomized them and their organization. Galvanized, they choreographed a sharing and commitment process throughout the company, which took another three months. The bedrock had been laid. It was then time to practice their new core values. They chose to anchor their organization on the following three of seven shared values and supporting norms.

PERSISTENCE: Tenacity to achieve the outcomes we expect that meet or exceed our standards.

Supporting norms: Hard work, energy, integrity, pride in work, and positive attitude.

FORWARD MOTION: Taking deliberate, adaptive, and/or motivating actions that draw on our inner spirit and tenacity in order to achieve a relevant objective, goal, or vision.

Supporting norms: Critical thinking, putting in necessary time, innovation, timeliness, and positive attitude.

COURAGEOUS TRUTH: Daring to remain authentic and true to our values when expressing our beliefs and/or making decisions, despite the consequences.

Supporting norms: Be clear and deliberate about what we do and why we do it, while displaying integrity, honesty, transparency, and being self-aware; be bold and ethical.

It is incumbent for leaders to display the resolve to change shared values, to define where the organization needs to shift its values and where it needs emphasis, assessing present values and the current external environment. To the point: is the CEO/C-suite, including founders and dominant shareholders, realistic about the values they are willing to espouse, and are these values relevant today, in light of their history and personal beliefs? The core values should create salience in order for the change initiative to gain serious attention; otherwise, your Da Vinci Organizational Code will falter. Change expectations will elusively evaporate.

Of course, disruption happens. Whether it was the time when a customer was dragged down the aisle of a commercial airline by a flight attendant, a product defect/design flaw covered up by the C-suite in an automotive company, a bank fleecing customers by enticing them to purchase unneeded products, poor quality driven by dirty rotten attitudes in service or product delivery, loyal suppliers being gouged on pricing, sexual misconduct, or unfair/inequitable compensation practices, the risk of inconsistency by leadership is formidable. Members of your organization who care might mentally check out, emotionally withdraw, and ultimately disappear, in search of a culture that aligns with their personal values.

Yet if shared and espoused values are consistently practiced, your enterprise will have a cornerstone or keystone that will be storm-worthy. A strongly aligned organization begins and ends with core values. That is the way it works.

2. STRATEGIC VISION

For effective alignment, the CEO, as well as other critical stakeholders, must be doggedly patient and persistent in their focus on creating a new set of shared values over the long term. This is what leads to successful strategic vision.

This vision is the formulated conviction of what has been achieved, what your organization is known for, and how you are now perceived. It is not about prediction but about preference.

To create a strategic vision, you must look back to analyze the results of hard work over a given period of time (usually, five years). You must recall and establish a reference point (e.g., during the first year) and vividly describe what has been achieved since then. Do not confuse strategic vision with strategy development and strategic planning (more discussion on the latter two subjects shortly). Strategic visioning is a process of preferring (a choice point) as opposed to predicting (a prognostication). It is a mental simulation, which visualizes the outcome of the end state.

Think of an Olympic diver. The competitor stands on the platform, steps out on the springboard, turns around, and comes back to the standing posture. Within that routine, the diver has envisioned the perfect dive, from the standing position to takeoff moment to angle of projection, velocity of the center of mass, and angular momentum, culminating in a perfect vertical and splash-less "rip entry" into the water—and to claiming the highest score. It is very precise and determined, similar to strategic visioning. This analogy combines both envisioning the end state and the specific steps to the end goal; a perfect dive.

I use the same process in one-on-one coaching. Whether it is a collective (organizational) and/or individual simulation, behaviors do change and organizational alignment is enhanced.

Here are some examples of strategic vision statements:

- "We are known as the employer of first choice in our industry, as measured by high employee retention, compensation, and profitability."
- "We are recognized in our community as a helper and supporter of safe streets and clean neighborhoods."
- "We have demonstrated that our products and services have out-performed our competitors' in quality satisfaction and customer acquisition."
- "The profitability of our company is significantly higher than that of our competitors."
- "Our compensation practices are aligned to our competitive position and profitability goal."
- "Our geographic expansion of distribution centers is over 100 with an employee base of 3,000."
- "Our new corporate headquarters is green-certified and eco-friendly, creating a spacious environment in which to connect, find solitude, and instill pride."

- "Our core values and strong culture ensure that our competitive advantage will be difficult to replicate by our competitors."

Once you have formulated the five-year strategic vision statement, assess your vision with the following questions. You may revise and modify your iteration after sharing it with employees and other critical stakeholders once you have received their feedback and input.

Five-Year Strategic Vision: Evaluation Discussion

The following questions highlight elements of the strategic- and human-centric systems foundational to Alignment Strong. The integration of these two mindsets is essential for an astute, strategic vision. Label each question with an **S** for **strategic-centric** and an **H** for **human-centric**. Do you see the balance in your vision statement? If not, where are the imbalance and distortion?

I. What Do You See and Feel?

- Does the vision statement convey a compelling picture of the enterprise in five years?
- What are the standout features that emotionally connect and give you relevance? Why?

II. How High Are You Going to Go?

- At the end of five years, will it be clear whether the vision has been achieved? Does it represent a clear, strategic direction?
- Is the opportunity to potentialize yourself apparent in this vision?

III. What Ways Can You Utilize It?

- Where does the vision statement intersect with employees, customers, competitors, suppliers, and community?
- Is the company's strategic posture and/or competitive advantage evidenced?

IV. Is It Me and Us?

- Does the vision statement build on the company's core values?
- Does it emphasize both empowerment and autonomy as well as organization-wide teamwork and cooperation?

V. Why Is This Important?

- Does it create a sense of belonging, hope, and excitement?
- Is organization-wide collaboration, trust, transparency, and caring apparent?

Most strategic vision statements are given voice in the boundless energy and youthful years of an organization's genesis and are a strong affirmation and reflection of the founder's core values and principles. In my executive coaching of CEOs, entrepreneurs, and other leaders, I find that without this component firmly in place and understood, there will be difficulties in achieving long-term sustainable results for leaders, employees, and the organization.

In those cases, a strategic re-visioning process is in order, which should result in a relevant, formulated, and engaging strategic vision statement. A strategic vision statement assists to create coherency and diminish fears among members of your organization of not knowing, not being involved in, or having little influence over the future. The sharing of this essential information helpfully reduces uncertainty and fear, and, as a result, the gnawing away of one's emotional commitment to the enterprise's mission.

Without an effective, formulated vision statement, strong organizational alignment is diminished. Your organization will not be postured to compete optimally. The company will exist without an essential component of its plumb line. It will be out of balance.

3. MISSION/COMPETITIVE ADVANTAGE

The formal mission, as evidenced in a statement, is an organization's wheelhouse: the most advantageous place, assuring shelter not only for the captain of the ship but for the rest of the organization as well. Without this very carefully worded paragraph that amplifies the competitive advantage, the enterprise will become submerged and sink. Without a mission, the organization will never take control of its own unique destiny, but someone else assuredly will. Unlike feel-good mantras such as "We are quality, period" or "We are just better," a sense of gravity and defensibility should be embodied in this sacrosanct declaration of an organization's mission. Its distillation and synthesis should emphasize the following:

- Prioritized internal and external customers/stakeholders that you will embrace or not embrace
- Prioritized and defined products and services that you will deliver (or not deliver) to identified customers
- Identified and defined standards/benchmarks for which you will hold yourself accountable in the delivery of products and services
- Rationalized and defined value proposition—the competitive advantage in which products and services are consistently delivered at a lower cost and/or demand a higher price, which your

rivals will struggle to match. Now defined, the pricing strategy has been more thoroughly rationalized. This cache of information is a critical component of the strategy and strategic plan.

To simplify this even more, the four priorities to address within a mission statement are as follows:

1. **Customers served**
2. **Products and services**
3. **Standard of delivery**
4. **Competitive advantage**

The first responsibility of top management is to ask, "What is our business?" Management consultant and author Peter Drucker not only posed this question and others in his classic text, *Management: Tasks, Responsibilities, Practices*, but cautioned that inadequate thought about business missions is perhaps the most important single cause of business frustration and business failure. After experiencing innumerable mission development sessions spanning forty years, I concur with Drucker. He stated, "To raise the question always reveals cleavages and differences within the top management group itself . . . The answer requires judgment and considerable courage. It never emerges as a logical conclusion from postulates or from facts. The answer rarely follows what 'everybody knows.' It should never be made on plausibility alone, never be made fast, never be made painlessly."[3]

Once you have defined products and services and underpinned a "quality excellence" description for each, including customer expectations, you must then perform a comparative analysis against your organization's top ten competitors. Ask the question, "How does my organization stack up per product and service against organizations that do not want to see us in the marketplace?" The resultant competitive analyses will further stimulate internal debate and external market inquiry, generating valuable insights that you can use in evaluating competitive posture (e.g., products/services mix, pricing, and market penetration) and formulating strategy assumptions.

With purposeful repetition, Drucker reenters the discussion with an admonition that once the enterprise attains its goals, it should always ask seriously, "What is our business?" and forewarns that "smugness, laziness, and arrogance are inevitably countered by such an inquiry when success does arrive."[4] Such conversation requires self-discipline and tenacity from the CEO. In my practice, when I have attempted to slow down top management to have these conversations, I have often been viewed as an obstructionist. Short-term tactical thinking seems to be so much more alluring than long-term priorities. In today's information overload and drive for top- and bottom-line growth, it is a conundrum requiring emotional self-control and a disciplined focus to do two things at the same time. The alternative is continued exposure to economic cycles and ultimate financial decline.

When you ask "What is our business?" you also need to add, "And what will it be? And how do we now build these anticipations into our theory of the business; into its strategies, goals, and work objectives?" Drucker further stresses, "What should our business be focusing on in the market, its potential, and its trends?"[5] This guy is merciless! Fast forward from Drucker wisdom, circa 1970s, to today's most recent mission—strategy theory, as pronounced by W. Chan Kim and Renée Mauborgne, who wrote *Blue Ocean Strategy: How to Create Uncontested Market Space and Make the Competition Irrelevant*. Wittingly or not, they supported Drucker's admonition as they delineated two strategies, labelling one Red Ocean and the other Blue Ocean. The Red Ocean focused on beating competitors in existing markets, while the Blue Ocean focused on generating new markets.[6] In a March 2020 *Harvard Business Review* article, "How to Achieve Resilient Growth Throughout the Business Cycle," they conclude: "We can all be the captain of our ship when we strike the right balance between market-competing and market-creating efforts. Red Ocean and Blue Ocean strategies are not a binary choice. Companies need both."[7] Forward motion is in play. Without it, you die. When you ask the previous questions posed by Drucker, agile learning is modeled, reinforcing an essential core value of the organization.

What follows is a real-life example integrating all four components of a mission statement. See if you can pick out the sentences that highlight customers served, products and services, standard of delivery, and competitive advantage.

HARVEY HOHAUSER & ASSOCIATES MISSION STATEMENT

"Extending its family legacy as a Michigan-based retained executive recruiting firm, Harvey Hohauser & Associates differentiates itself through the placement of strategically adaptive and culturally aligned executives. We are trusted advisors and partners, committed to providing values-based expert consultative services to private and public companies and the professional community. Our process engages a global network, deep market knowledge, selection excellence, timeliness, and integrity. We are founded on and thrive in creating and sustaining genuine long-term relationships that provide opportunity and added value for our clients, candidates, and the greater global community."

Did you find the phrases that fit each essential component that must be included in a mission statement? I've listed them below:

1. **Customers served:** "private and public companies and the professional community"
2. **Products and services:** "deep market knowledge, selection excellence, timeliness, and integrity"

3. **Standard of delivery:** "providing values-based expert consultative services"

4. **Competitive advantage:** "placement of strategically adaptive and culturally aligned executives"

Development of the statement, formulation of a competitive analysis matrix, and the final evaluation and sign-off by four members of this enterprise took six months to complete. Don't let the brevity of the statement fool you. There was intense discourse and verbal bloodletting over all of the components. For instance, the "products and services" portion comprised six pages of definitions and quality performance measurements. Besides grinning, Drucker would have a high regard for this enterprise's effort. I am hopeful that their mission formulation increases qualified, top-line revenue and net profit margins, in light of the other nine components of Alignment Strong that this company was also undertaking.

In Appendix item 2 you will find a **Mission Statement Development Procedure and Evaluation** to help you shape and critique your organization's expressed mission.

4. LEADERSHIP/TEAM

The CEO must guide and motivate his or her team with espoused values and a compelling strategic vision. A leader must be open to embrace personal development. A strongly aligned organization demands leadership adaptability to changing situations and competitive landscapes, which is underscored by the openness to examine one's own management and decision-making style effectiveness. By taking a deep dive into yourself, your filters and blind spots become clearer. When you exemplify vulnerability, you also build trust within your organization; psychological safety is established with the executive team.

The book *Primal Leadership* by Goleman, Boyatzis, and McKee made the point that "if climate drives business results, what drives climate? Roughly 50 to 70 percent of how employees perceive their organization's climate can be traced to the actions of one person: the leader. More than anyone else, the boss creates the conditions that directly determine people's ability to work well."[8] And as Bjorn Christian Martinoff, a best-selling author and top global leadership authority, has noted, "Leadership is the ability to channel and increase energy toward a purpose and vision while being guided by values."[9]

Here's a baseline question I pose to CEOs in the sensing phase, before we mutually agree upon a formal coaching engagement: "Do you feel your leadership and your commitment are felt and visible throughout the organization?"

The initial response to this question is telling. A leader can fudge it, and conclude that his or her leadership and commitment are somewhat felt and visible. But to get an accurate picture, we can employ the "Credibility Leaders' Guide" developed by James Kouzes and Barry Posner, authors of the book *Credibility: How Leaders Gain and Lose It, Why People Demand It*. Using the statements below, assess your credibility:

1. My decisions and actions are consistent; they reflect and clearly communicate my personal values.

   ALWAYS   **OFTEN**   **RARELY**

2. I am accessible and respond to the questions and concerns of my constituents honestly and in a timely manner.

   ALWAYS   **OFTEN**   **RARELY**

3. I make time to meet with my constituents on a face-to-face basis, and have familiarized myself with what is involved in each of their jobs.

   ALWAYS   **OFTEN**   **RARELY**

4. My decisions take into consideration input from my constituents. I decide by building consensus.

ALWAYS   **OFTEN**   **RARELY**

5. I foster a feeling of cooperation and community among my constituents.

ALWAYS   **OFTEN**   **RARELY**

6. I provide opportunities for my constituents to learn and grow in their jobs.

ALWAYS   **OFTEN**   **RARELY**

7. I have created a work environment where my constituents are free to make decisions on their own, learn from each other, and experiment.

ALWAYS   **OFTEN**   **RARELY**

8. I hold myself to the same standards as my constituents and try to set a positive example in all aspects of our relationship.

ALWAYS   **OFTEN**   **RARELY**

9. I see my job as one of empowerment; I credit my constituents whenever possible and create heroes in my organization, beginning with my team.

ALWAYS   **OFTEN**   **RARELY**

10. I am honest in acknowledging problems, but focus on solving the problems, and try to stay flexible and promote optimism and faith in a successful outcome among my constituents.[10]

ALWAYS   **OFTEN**   **RARELY**

Reflecting on your assessment, an absence or infrequency of "Always/Often" indicates that improvement is in order. This brief analysis is by no means exhaustive, yet it is insightful and should encourage you to look deeper into the subject of credibility and the leader's impact on organizational climate and financial results.

The Power of a Leader

The leader's impact is really about the leader's personal power. Nothing reveals what a person in a leadership position is all about like power. I have observed a great number of CEOs handle misfortune, and qualities of leadership character can become evident in such situations. But I get a very different glimpse of what a CEO is really about once he or she has attained power. These leaders have a tendency either to be more consumed by themselves (selfishness) or exhibit a naiveté, capsulized by the cogitation, "Now that I have power, what exactly is it, and what do I do with it?" Surprisingly, the majority of CEOs I have worked with fall into the latter category, which borders on role ambivalence and role ambiguity. Temperaments vary as well on this scale, from self-grandiosity and invincibility on one pole to self-rejection and vincibility on the other.

Where do you lie on the personal power continuum? Do you find yourself too overpowering or too underpowering? Regardless of our position, very few of us have been tutored in this topic.

The subject of power is a touchy area for most CEOs. This domain is infrequently discussed and rarely understood in the context of leadership effectiveness. Usually, my inquiry leads to a shallow, safe, general, moral, and philosophical discourse. The English historian, politician, writer, and great all-around personality of the nineteenth century, Lord Acton, famously admonished, "Absolute power corrupts absolutely." CEOs often recite this quote to me, trying to convey that "I know what this means and I am not that way," and with a sigh they will continue with something such as, "I disdain people in trusted positions who have gone awry. I am fortunate. I'm not that way. Can we change the subject now?" With restraint, I typically respond with, "Hold on there," and encourage them to extend the conversation.

Accordingly, the word "power" has been sugar-coated with Hollywood imagery to encapsulate ideas such as inspiration, impact, influence, charisma. To have a CEO identify and own his or her power, to understand how it impacts others and be able to use it effectively, is a worthy task. "Power" is laden with deep beliefs, labels, misperceptions, and conditioned responses. So let's bore a little deeper.

By choice, your power can be used to get or achieve what you want for personal gain and/or recognition—which contains all the markings of the signature high achiever—or it can be used to get others what *they* need, putting the welfare of others and the purpose of the organization before your own personal agenda. The latter has all the markings of a servant leader, and this refreshing mantra emanates from some C-suites today.

Power doesn't have to corrupt. It does not have to be abused. Nor must you avoid using it. Power can be a positive, affirming force that an effective leader can use to impact people. Whether the style of its expression is affiliative (built on authentic social relationships), authoritative (founded on reliability), or competitive (demonstrated by high achievement), power impacts others. Akin to a charge of dynamite, it can jar an organization into forward motion toward a chosen destination. Power is an essential ingredient within an integrated culture and an Alignment Strong enterprise. To see a leader deftly, consciously, and situationally employ all three styles—affiliative, authoritative, and competitive—is to witness an art form.

In my mid-thirties, we built our real estate investment trust organization, enabling investors to buy individual shares in real estate/real estate financing instruments, to approximately $100 million in assets with an equity base of $10 million. This was pre-Nasdaq. We were listed "over the counter" (OTC). My company hit its first significant recession when the prime rate soared to 21.5 percent. I was full of bravado and invincibility, but now that I was being tested, I began to feel the loss of self-confidence. Fear seeped into my psyche and my stomach churned.

One evening, my neighbor tenant, Robert Evans, former chairman of American Motors (then maker of the Jeep), and his friend, Warren Avis (founder of Avis Rent-a-Car), were consoling me on an elevator and persuaded me to have a drink with them at the Renaissance Club, located at the Renaissance Center, now the world headquarters of General Motors. This club was also the hangout for Henry Ford (the deuce), another one of their acquaintances. Walking into the club, I felt a reverence percolating. Being in the presence of elders seems to do that. After we sat down, sensing I was emotionally disheveled, they asked more about my plight and then assured me that this challenge was to be expected. They even snickered, saying it was okay to go as far as to have a nervous breakdown. The two claimed they had, usually on remote beaches. Hearing that, I was forlorn and agitated. Convinced a meltdown of this magnitude would not befall me, I moved forward in denial and invulnerability.

But the genesis of the unfreezing of my ego germinated, morphing me from one end of the power continuum to another. My ego was sufficiently contracted by the eventual turnaround and narrow survival of my own enterprise. My fall from invincibility permitted a humility and empathy to emanate within me. My power repertoire was enlarged. Affirmation found a significant foothold in my role as CEO and in my personal life, displacing a good chunk of my arrogance and invulnerability. I evolved into a more effective CEO. The company grew to nearly $450 million in assets and $28 million in equity over the next five years, with uninterrupted quarterly cash dividends for eleven straight years. Yet future personal power experiences were down the highway, stretching me to learn new lessons.

Sometime later, psychologist Colin Horn, PhD, who specializes in group dynamics and interpersonal communication analysis, shared his paper on "Types of Power and Their Manifestations" with me, and I have used his framework in my coaching practice. Colin is a very helpful and approachable person. His methodology is user-friendly and draws the participant in, to converse about a sensitive subject in a non-threatening way. With simplicity, he labels and characterizes three impact categories, bringing clarity to the subject of power. In the passages below, in #1 and #2, I have complemented the descriptors with the "leadership derailers" **(please note the asterisks)** described in Dotlich and Cairo's book *Why CEOs Fail*, and in #3 with the essential "social intelligence competences" for effective leadership prescribed in Daniel Goleman and Richard Boyatzis's article "Social Intelligence and the Biology of Leadership." Now, in my consulting work, I will first ask a CEO to tell me how others, beginning with his or her C-suite members, would describe how that CEO impacts them. Then I share Horn's framework with my client, asking if one of the following categories comes reasonably close to their own self-description.

1. **Abusive impact**—You dominate and drive fear and insecurity into your followers to get things done. Other descriptors: *Arrogant. Doesn't listen. *Volatility. Blaming. Negative. Interrupt. Dictating. *Perfectionism. Ordering. Ridicules. *Eccentricity. Passive-aggressive. *Mischievousness. Double bind. Bully. Bulldozer. *Melodrama (moody).

2. **Avoidance impact**—You are afraid/reticent to own and use your power. Other descriptors: Placate. White lies. Agree when disagree. *Excessive caution. False compliments. Insecure. Laissez-faire. Avoid conflict. *Aloofness. Flatterer, suck-up. *Eagerness to please. Don't want to approach others. Afraid/uncomfortable to hold subordinates accountable. *Habitual distrust. [11]

3. **Affirmation impact**[12]—You esteem others for their effort, for what they know as opposed to what they don't know, and yet you are clear and firm about performance expectations. Other

descriptors: *Empathy. *Attunement. Give help. Mutual respect. *Inspiration. Easy to approach. Self-revealing. Direct. Give honest feedback. Coach (*developing others). Empower. *Teamwork. Thankful for help. Disagree openly. *Organizational awareness.[13]

Labeling these three impact buckets really brings clarity into the conversation. The CEOs I work with usually become quite focused, begin to ponder, retreat into self-reflection, and then cautiously answer with something such as, "I hope number 3, but more than likely, I'm somewhere between number 1 and number 2 and have some attributes of number 3."

The critical insight I am conveying is this: It is not about identifying the dominant bucket in this power repertoire, although this is useful, but the lack of self and social awareness one has about their own personal power. As a leader, you could remedy this. Look inside yourself. Give time to insight and self-reflection. Your organization either sees and feels your influence or it doesn't, and if it does, what does it see and feel? How do you impact people with your personal power? Where do you need to move the needle, behaviorally? From what to what? Now use what I gave you in Chapter 2 under the subhead **The Change Formula**. What are the first/next steps to acquire new knowledge, to practice/exemplify the leadership style and temperament that is required?

Building an Effective Team

Ideally, the commitment to evolve into a more effective leader, including the use of personal power, supports a team-building process that will render more tangible results. Appropriately, an organization should use a proven, sound developmental model and team assessment, which I have included as Appendix item 6. This will be foundational to evaluate team mission, role, procedures, resources, performance, relationships, and organization, and will edify the leader's skills, self-confidence, and team commitment. The hallmark of a strong leader is the capability to build an effective team. The team is the reflection of the leader. It is the vehicle to attaining strategic vision.

Google, in an internal study called Aristotle (it must be erudite), spent two years scrutinizing 180 teams, and concluded five traits hallmarked the most successful ones. The codification of Google's secrets to team effectiveness is summarized by Michael Schneider, a human capital specialist. He cites findings by Google analytics leader Julia Rozovsky that the five top traits for team effectiveness are as follows.[14]

1. **Dependability:** Team members get things done on time and meet expectations.

2. **Structure and clarity:** High-performing teams have clear goals, and have well-defined roles within the group.

3. **Meaning:** The work has personal significance to each member.

4. **Impact:** The group believes their work is purposeful and positively impacts the greater good.

5. **Psychological safety:** This trait stood out from the rest. We've all been in meetings and, due to the fear of seeming incompetent, have held back questions or ideas. I get it. It's unnerving to feel like you're in an environment where everything you do or say is under a microscope. But imagine a different setting. A situation in which everyone is safe to take risks, voice opinions, and ask judgment-free questions. A culture where managers provide air cover and create safe zones so employees can let down their guard. That's psychological safety.

   In many organizations, top traits 1 through 4 are at least readily recognized and often fulfilled to a significant degree. But, in part because of the high positiveness of team members who are good at 1 through 4, number 5 is more difficult to address and honor.

Yet without psychological safety, the Alignment Strong process will be hard pressed to engage organizational members fully. Psychological safety creates the right climate temperature, affirming a manifestation of the ethos of the enterprise ("we are transparent with one another and feel safe here"), founded on the organization's shared and espoused values, now extended into the external environment. This inward-to-outward process builds brand trust. It has to. Deep integrity exudes inside and seeps outside the enterprise into the marketplace.

A recent example of psychological safety at play: I observed a client CEO open up a monthly team session with a "check-in" question: "How are you feeling today as we move into this agenda?" Everyone answered and he was the last team member to comment. Unknowingly, he paraphrased the transition author Elisabeth Kübler-Ross: "I am not okay today, and you don't have to be okay today, and that's okay." Within that moment, I observed and felt a sigh of relief from seven other members as we moved into a very technical, cross-functional, annual goal-setting ratification team session. Their respected leader had allowed them to feel psychologically safe; to be "not okay."

Melting the Iceberg

When Kimberley Barker—who wrote the Foreword to this book—and I discussed current organization development theory, she shared meaningful insights from consultant Sidney Yoshida's legendary 1989 study, "The Iceberg of Ignorance." His conclusions on the organizational plight of disengagement decades ago rattled the business and academic communities, and now reinforce the criticality of employee engagement in Alignment Strong.

Barker finds that Yoshida's "Iceberg of Ignorance" is quite relevant today. In essence, Yoshida said that frontline workers know 100 percent of the problems happening in an organization, their supervisors are aware of 74 percent of the problems, middle managers are aware of 9 percent, and senior leadership/executives are aware of only 4 percent—only the tip of the iceberg![15] You might quibble with the exact numbers, but there seems to be no doubt that frontline employees are keen to what is going right and wrong in the organization and yet senior leaders rarely engage them on their thoughts about how to move the organization forward.

Barker asserts that executives who practice servant/humble/compassionate leadership know the secrets to melting the iceberg. These leaders know that they do not have to have all of the answers, and they seek to engage employees at all levels and hear their suggestions. Employees do not want to know that you have implemented every one of their ideas. What they do want to know is whether they have been heard and that their ideas are being considered for your practices, roles, and processes. They need to feel psychologically safe enough to come to you as their leader with their ideas and observations.

Vulnerability

Psychological safety does not come easy. Leaders have a choice to either create the psychological safety or not. If they do, employees will begin to exhibit acts of vulnerability. This behavior will set an example and others will try it on for size. The boss—and ideally, peers—should then show affirmation and reinforcement so that the risk was worth the reward. The Latin origin for vulnerability is *vulnerare*. It means "to wound." This willful act takes loads of courage. Pause for a moment and ask: "Who in their right mind wants to consciously wound himself or herself?" All of us weigh out the act of being vulnerable as opposed to being invulnerable. We cautiously calculate the risk versus the reward. Self-talk kicks in: "Does the reward exceed the risk of being misunderstood, feeling clumsy, admitting mistakes, seeking forgiveness that may not be received, or not being affirmed?"

I recall on numerous occasions, while building a coffee company with my wife in the remote rainforest of Papua New Guinea, spears being thrown at my feet or being confronted by conniving sorcerers or clans bearing machetes. I felt like soiling my pants on those occasions. I did not consider this a sign of weakness but an indication that I was a human and feeling weak at the moment. It was a sign of my being vulnerable. That is strength. Being exposed is not a learned behavior. In fact, much of my life was devoted to building a significant fortress to safeguard my exposure. It has taken a great deal of stamina to counter this effort—hopefully an indicator of a sustained growth mindset as opposed to a fixed mindset.

Most leaders I have coached know this feeling of fear. They correlate the feeling of being vulnerable to not being in control. But without the attribute of vulnerability beginning with and resonating from the boss, though not necessarily to a pants-soiling extreme, refuge (psychological safety) will not be created. A leader's emotional empathy has to be evidenced by the sheer acts of vulnerability (your willingness to emotionally expose yourself) to connect authentically with another person.

Catching myself, after authoring so many pages on component # 4, I realize the subject of Leadership/Team continues to elude me. Why? My adult life struggle remains centered on a seemingly impenetrable blind spot labeled personal power. This still has a hold on me. Continually, I probe myself to gain greater comprehension. Often I do this by asking the question, How am I impacting this coachee? Evolving oneself is pretty demanding and definitely intimate work. With consolation, I remind John Quinlan that it is a work in progress. I do the same thing with my clients. In fact, I have a very high positive regard for my coachees, assuming they are motivated and are emotionally committed to the change they envision. I trust that the regard I have for them is felt and seen.

Just like you, I want to be seen and felt as an affirmative human being. May I venture to say I am mirroring you and you are mirroring me? Does this sound familiar?

I come back to this: In your evolving leadership role, as you are charged with the responsibility to build a high-performing team, psychological safety, articulated by vulnerability, makes sense. Without such safety, the unfreezing of yourself and the iceberg called your organization may not happen. The group may simply deflect our change formula and remain untransformed. Let's keep the human centric system in mind as we now move on to the rationalistic and strategic system of Alignment Strong.

5. STRATEGY

This component begins with formulating and articulating a rational/logical strategic narrative for the company's supporting goals and objectives. Usually the strategy narrative has a lifespan of one to two years and is the responsibility of the CEO and his or her team to formulate. It should not be delegated to the CFO. This goes for the strategic plan as well. This narrative development is a group effort and should include the following.

Strategy Tests

Strategy Test 1. Leveraging off mission development and competitive analysis, you now have clarification to ascertain whether your value proposition is different enough to underpin your strategy. Joan Magretta wrote a concise book about Michael Porter, known for his theories on economics, business strategy, and social causes, as well as for creating his "five forces analysis," which is instrumental in business strategy development. In *Understanding Michael Porter*, Magretta states, "The first test of a strategy is whether your value proposition is different from your rivals. If you are trying to serve the same customers and meet the same needs and sell at the same relative price, then by Porter's definition, you don't have a strategy."[16]

Strategy Test 2. Magretta emphasizes that the second test of a sound strategy is whether your value chain is tailored to meet customer needs (e.g., from a customer inquiry to final invoice). Do your internal activities/links deliver products and services differently than your competitors? She further comments, "Porter's logic is simple and compelling. If it were not the case, every competitor could meet the same needs, and there would be nothing unique or valuable about the positioning."[17]

Parallel to missioning, strategy development can be a challenging process. But you simply need to apply these two strategy tests. Put these two components of a strategy narrative on paper—or on your computer—and defend them. The resulting consensus should be articulated in a strategy narrative no more than two to three pages long, using complete paragraphs—as well as bullet points—to drive home salient points (e.g., relevance, significance, degree), which is always open to revision.

A strategy narrative is a work in process, both deliberate/rationalistic and organic/emergent.

Henry Mintzberg, a Canadian academic and author on business and management, clarifies: "The strategy-making process should be capturing what the manager learns from all sources: soft insights from his/her personal experiences and experiences of others . . . hard data from market research and the like. Then synthesizing that learning into a vision of the direction that business should pursue."[18]

You will build the narrative with critical assumptions, including culture, environment, operations, and financial. These premises are open to constant assessment and revision as well. Strategy integrates the demand and supply side of the business. When a strategy is crafted, as purported by Michael Porter, "it gives comprehension on how a company, faced with competition, will out-compete its rivals."[19] Over the long term, a company will achieve sustainable competitive advantage if the strategic narrative, along with the other nine components of the Da Vinci Organizational Code, is developed and integrated.

Robert S. Kaplan and David P. Norton concisely articulate in their 2008 online *Harvard Business Review* article, "Mastering the Management System," the following questions; the answers should be vetted as part of the strategy narrative.

- Which customers or markets will we target?
- What is the value proposition that distinguishes us?
- What key processes give us competitive advantage?
- What are the human capital capabilities required to excel at these key processes?
- What are the technology enablers of the strategy?
- What are the organizational enablers required for the strategy?[20]

In summary, books and texts about strategy are often too abstract to be pragmatically grasped. They can be tedious reads. I have attempted to take a very complex but essential subject and break it down in the preceding discussion and concluding points, in order for you to comprehend and capture the significant role that strategy plays in the alignment process. You may want to seek out the texts of all the authors I have cited in this strategy discussion for more information. They are masters in their fields. I thank them for their contributions.

Keep in mind that textbooks, mapping processes, *Harvard Business Review* case studies, McKinsey research-founded articles, PWC/

Accenture strategy surveys, and others do not take the place of having good conversations with team members. If you attempt anything, take the preceding questions and sequester yourself with your top team and let it fly.

6. GOALS/OBJECTIVES

Goals and objectives are the outcomes of comprehensive strategic planning. And yes, you would expect to achieve this end by distilling SWOT and PESTLE analyses. Included in this data collection would be a further examination of your own industry. By incorporating Michael Porter's *Five Forces* industry assessment (e.g., competitors, new entrants, customers, suppliers, substitution threat of products and services), you will increase the breadth and depth of your external environment planning assumptions for competitive posture.[21]

The results of the SWOT (Strengths, Weaknesses, Opportunities, and Threats) and PESTLE (Political, Economic, Social, Technological, Legal, and Environmental) analyses will help you to leverage internal strengths and external opportunities, and mitigate internal weaknesses and external threats into precise, strategic issue definitions. Accordingly, you will develop goals and objectives (action steps) to resolve the strategic issues. Then, integrate your pro forma, highlighting projected sales/revenue, gross profit margin, and a net profit target, and include that with the balance sheet and cash flow plan, inclusive of a capital expenditures budget (Cap Ex schedule). With all this assembled, now go back to assumption testing to flesh out the best, expected, and worst-case scenarios with your team. The finished and team-ratified document is the annual strategic business plan.

The goal-setting process will motivate people—beginning with the C-suite and waterfalling down into the organization—to execute the plan. Extensive research evidence shows that goal setting can be used to motivate people to perform more effectively (Latham & Yukl, 1975).[22]

The same research concludes that there must be three conditions for effective goal setting.

1. **The goals that are set must be clear and specific.** The employee must understand each goal precisely.

2. **The goals should be challenging.** Goals that motivate are hard to achieve but are reachable. Goals that are too easily realized will obviously not motivate high performance; goals that are far too difficult to reach will be considered impossible and likely to motivate the employee to simply give up without trying.

3. **Individuals should participate in setting their own goals.** This participation may increase their commitment to the goals because the objectives in this case will more likely fit with the subordinates' own levels of aspiration. Additionally, participation may simply help the individual to understand the goal more clearly, or to see it as an achievable end (Sashkin, 1982).[23]

    Whatever the reason, participation does seem to help people achieve their goals, especially in the long run. You should note, however, that participation is not an absolute requirement. Research indicates that even non-participatory goal setting can be effective in motivating employees to perform better. When all three factors are present—clear goals, challenging goals, and participative goals—motivation will be at its highest in the goal-setting process.

Ideally, your organization's goal-setting process has met the preceding criteria. A team may then utilize a goal ratification procedure, further emboldening members to cross over into other functions, roles, and departments. This will help their teammates and the organization by providing input and personal feedback to the champion/coordinator of each goal, thereby assuring more accurate goals and action plans. The team will begin to realize heroics are not mandatory. It's not about ego. Failures and mishaps will certainly occur. Accuracy will become the most dynamic learning objective. It is all about accuracy.

The importance of "results-focused experimental learning" cannot be overstated, as specified by business consultant and author Robert H. Schaffer. He comments that "Little learning occurs . . . in organizations that do not have frequent experience in setting tough goals and then mobilizing their wits and energies to achieve them."[24] I have included an example of a completed **Strategic Issue Definition, Goal Statement and Objectives/Action Steps**, and a **Goal/Action Plan Team Ratification Session** template as Appendix items 7 and 8 to assist you in this learning process.

The goal/objective-setting process waterfalls into all departments and finally, into individual roles. This alignment links the bottom to the top macro goals of the company as well as the current strategy. The reward system then becomes more relevant and linked to results, as evidenced by the successful execution/completion of the action plans.

Accountability

Beginning with the CEO, demand management (holding people accountable) is an imperative once an effective goal-setting process is in place. Effective leaders and managers are expected to possess the capability and fortitude to hold/demand another person accountable to values, behaviors, goals, and objectives. Year after year, I use my **Leadership Development Questionnaire** (Appendix item 3) to assess a CEO's learning priorities and then co-develop a curriculum with them. Invariably, the ability to hold another person accountable is in the top ten desired skills for a leader, along with effective conflict resolution skills.

Yes, it is necessary to have a work plan, with a timetable, and to review goal progress regularly. Let's check how you rate yourself on holding others accountable by using a clever assessment developed by Robert H. Schaffer, author of *High-Impact Consulting*. Do any of the following statements ring true?

Demand Management Assessment[25]

	ALWAYS	SOMETIMES	NEVER
1. I insist on written work plans that state how people will achieve their goals.			
2. I review progress regularly.			
3. My people believe that there are significant consequences for success or failure.			
4. I forcefully confront people when projects go astray.			

Now, what can you do with the results of this assessment? If your evaluation indicates you are effective ("always" to all four) in holding subordinates accountable, then make sure your managers are doing the same thing and it will waterfall through the organization. If you fall short (mixed bag of "sometimes" and "never"), then address this deficiency very soon. Your lack of ability to hold others accountable is demotivating employees and costing you a lot in time, assets, knowledge, and capital.

Take the time to further evaluate your leadership and management skills. Determine your top ten learning priorities. (The **Leadership Development Questionnaire**—Appendix item 3—provides a specific exercise for doing this.) Solicit feedback from your board, peers, team, affinity group, coach and/or trusted advisor to examine your own conclusions, assumptions, and potential blind spots once you have completed the questionnaire.

By using these strategic planning and goal-setting tools and through systematic evaluation of your skills (e.g., demand management) as a leader, you can strengthen your organization exponentially. With this sixth component in place, you want to make sure your enterprise has a relevant and adaptive organization structure. Now, let's progress to the seventh component of the Da Vinci Organizational Code.

7. ORGANIZATION STRUCTURE

The organizational structure of an enterprise is the infrastructure (skeleton) that facilitates information flow, communications, accountability, and efficient work processes. It is also open to question. Once you've defined purpose, strategy, mission, and goals, it is logical to assess if the current organization structure is optimal and if it is effectively adapting to the external environment. According to researchers in 2013, "When business problems emerge, signs often exist within the design or components of the organizational structure. In some cases, these signs can be early indicators of significant problems that need to be addressed." They go on to describe "The Signs of Poor Organization Structure:"[26]

- **Low productivity**

  A low rating in this key metric can indicate a problem in an organization's structure, such as inefficient resource allocation, poor vertical communication, or employee empowerment constraints. Employees may lack the proper environment to complete their work assignments efficiently.

- **Unequal workload**

  Poor organizational structure can result in an unequal distribution of work among departments or divisions. When some areas of a company are routinely understaffed and must work overtime while other areas struggle to find sufficient work to keep every employee busy, the organizational structure has not been optimized.

- **Lines of communication unclear**
  Employees who routinely bypass the standard chain of command could be a sign of poor organizational design. Employees with complaints or suggestions should typically provide feedback to their direct manager or occasionally to their manager's boss. In an optimal business, employees should feel their voices are heard through the standard management path. In an organization with a poor structure, employees may feel the need to go directly to a department head, vice president, or even the president to express concerns or recommendations.

- **Lack of teamwork**
  Bad organizational structure does little to foster teamwork. Departments may be unwilling or unable to cooperate with each other. Workers may not feel a sense of camaraderie, and thus focus on their individual tasks without offering assistance to others.

- **Slow decision making**
  Slow decisions can hamper sales opportunities and innovations. Structural change may be necessary if an organization does not direct decision-making authority to the appropriate person, or issues must travel through multiple layers of management before a result is rendered. A leaner, more focused decision-making process may foster an innovative spirit in the company.

- **Lack of innovation**
  Companies with bad organizational structure are often slow to innovate. A pipeline for new ideas may not exist, or it might not lead to the right source for development and implementation.

Consequently, workers who come up with new ideas may keep them to themselves or take them to a new employer.

An organization that has pondered the preceding symptoms would be able to ascertain more strategic answers to the following questions I have developed and listed.

Organizational Structure Inquiry

- Does the current structure support the delivery of competitive advantage and the ethos of customer-centricity? If yes, please defend your response.
- Does the present structure support or impede the organization's value chain optimization? If your answer is "support," please explain. If not, where in the value chain are the obvious disconnects/bottlenecks/ duplications impacted by the organization structure?
- Are roles and reporting relationships clearly defined and rationalized within the organization structure? In thirty-three years of organization assessments, I have never had more than 60 percent respond with "yes."
- Is the structure adaptive and swift enough to capture opportunities and mitigate threats in the external marketplace? Please explain how it does capture this information and how it is used, including the decision-making process.
- Is the organization structured for optimal effectiveness and efficiency? Please prove it.
- Is the organization structured to make itself "easy to do business with"? What are the criteria you measure this with and how do you use the measurements?

The critical question:

- Is the leader's temperament, management practices, and decision-making style reflective, open, adaptive, and "ego-contained," responsive to both the organization's culture and its operating environment in order to readily and speedily reconfigure/modify the organization structure in times of certainty or uncertainty?

Accordingly, when one literally or virtually puts pen to paper to sketch out a structural framework, one of three configurations may emerge: a functional structure, a product/service/program structure, or a mixture of both—a matrix structure. One of these may rationalize an optimal design for the organization. Frequently, to create the optimal organizational structure—the structural sweet spot—for the company, the stability and predictability of function structure are integrated with the highly focused expertise, interdependency, and flexibility of the product/service/program structure. You may even evolve to a more ad hoc culturally and customer-centric structure, a mutation of all three.

Keep in mind that the matrix organization structure demands high coordination, exemplary management skills, and consistent accountability processes.

Nevertheless, the end goal is a comprehension for the rationale of the organization structure.

The organization structure encompasses a collection of departmental units and subcultures. It can be viewed as a community. Ideally, they are now structured organization-wide to effectively and efficiently discharge their individual missions executing the internal value chain of the organization. These departmental missions will support the corporate mission statement, which we addressed in component number three. We will now move this discussion to component number eight.

8. DEPARTMENTAL MISSION STATEMENTS/VALUE CHAIN

Functional statements developed by individual departments such as engineering, production, accounting, IT, HR, purchasing, marketing/sales, and others reflect their commitment to—and operationalization/execution of—the corporate mission statement. The formulation of these statements follows the same process as the corporate mission statement. It is imperative that these functional mission statements identify their specific outputs/deliverables as internal vendors and linkages in the internal value chain and in support of the corporate mission statement. Examples of these deliverables would be timely and accurate drawings from engineering, exact production schedules from manufacturing, relevant financial metrics to keep score—dashboard—from accounting, proactive and relevant training from IT, a defined onboarding process from HR, competitively priced equipment from purchasing, qualified/vetted customer expectations from marketing and sales, and so on. These outputs would be coupled to critical responsibilities captured in the defined roles for each departmental team member. Consequently, departmental team members should be able to clearly define and comprehend their roles and reporting relationships, eliminating role ambiguity and role conflict, critical for high performance.

Again, identifying the departmental value chain's inputs-through-puts-outputs will assist in identifying the internal and external disconnects and bottlenecks within and between departments. This must be followed by corrective actions (e.g., standard operating procedures, quality protocols, interpersonal skills development, resolution of existing conflicts within and outside the department).

More value added (MVA: innovating/thinking/creating) can also germinate actions to enhance the outputs (products/services) as a handoff to the next link (the internal customer) in the value chain. This process will drive integrity into the department's mission, as team members would begin to execute at a higher performance level. Everyone wins: the departmental team, the organization-wide value chain, and the customer.

Bakery Department Value Chain

The following example is a hypothetical department created by one of my clients, a custom, design-precision engineered machinery company. The member of the company leading the value chain optimization initiative attained a PhD in IT. He chose a bakery department to illustrate how one department within an organization-wide value chain can be impactful. Such simplification is a wonderful skill. I've used this illustration for both disconnect/bottleneck analysis and MVA innovation sessions with other companies.

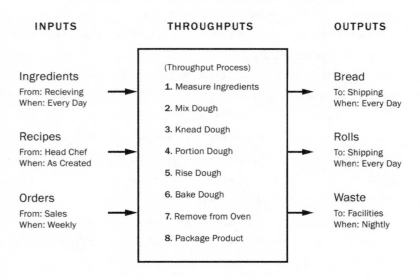

BAKERY DEPARTMENT VALUE CHAIN

INPUTS	THROUGHPUTS	OUTPUTS
Ingredients From: Recieving When: Every Day	(Throughput Process) 1. Measure Ingredients 2. Mix Dough	**Bread** To: Shipping When: Every Day
Recipes From: Head Chef When: As Created	3. Knead Dough 4. Portion Dough 5. Rise Dough	**Rolls** To: Shipping When: Every Day
Orders From: Sales When: Weekly	6. Bake Dough 7. Remove from Oven 8. Package Product	**Waste** To: Facilities When: Nightly

Using a framework like this one to illustrate and examine a value chain can assist in identifying disconnects/bottlenecks and generating solutions.

Hypothetically, the bakery team in this example now comprehends and agrees to their value chain diagram. They understand the inputs, throughputs, and outputs. They comprehend the interdependency of both the socio (soft-side) requirements and technical (hard-side) requirements of their department and individual roles. They realize the company has to immediately adapt to the external environment (ecosystem), by swiftly receiving and utilizing critical feedback from both outside and inside the company. In fact, they have received recent negative feedback on quality, timeliness, and attitudes from two other departments.

The bakery team convened and addressed the social-interpersonal issues (i.e., bad attitudes, defensiveness, empowerment ambivalence, management slackness), as well as technical/quality/product specification issues. The team leader did an effective job identifying both the soft and hard concerns. Now let's make an educated guess. What percent of the issues were soft side versus the hard side? In this case, 70 percent were soft-side issues versus 30 percent hard-side issues. Were you surprised?

After practicing value chain optimization for thirty years, I've found that problem areas usually are between 60 and 80 percent on the soft side. Accordingly, examining the bakery department's throughput steps (internal workflow) revealed the disconnects and bottlenecks within their own department. The team developed action plans to address both soft- and hard-side issues that would be reviewed at the next session. The team convened another meeting to brainstorm/innovate on critical inputs that would impact customer perceptions of the company at large to value add. They concluded they needed to affirm the core values of the company by aligning their attitudes and work habits, as well as to examine their ingredients to make their product healthier and easily digestible, more appealing and marketable.

They set new metrics to begin baking bread earlier in order to ship orders out earlier, and to ship rolls out daily. They also streamlined procedures to eliminate waste, and they established metrics to measure the impact of more effective mixing, kneading, and oven efficacy. But what excited them the most was their idea to improvise the use of "wasted dough" into signature, chocolate-covered pretzels as well as breadsticks. A cost benefits and market study began, which included evaluating strategic alliances with a well-known chocolate candy producer across town and a chain of Italian restaurants statewide that wanted a better breadstick product than they currently received from a competitor.

The execution (epitomized operational excellence) of linked horizontal, organization-wide mission statements would assure the delivery of competitive advantage. The execution of those functional missions would exemplify an organization-wide integrated team.

Michael Hammer, in his book *The Agenda*, labels this collective effort "the extended value chain," which extends one's internal value chain to include customers and suppliers.[27] This results in MVA and easy-to-do-business-with (ETDBW) outcomes. In order to deliver more value added, Hammer stresses that the following more comprehensive and transcending questions should be asked: "What do our customers do with our products and services after they have received them from us? What are the broader business or personal problems they may have? What more can we do to help them solve these problems?" For instance, imagine if the airline industry would go through such an inquiry and self-examination.

Being able to answer these questions and then doing whatever it takes to deliver your commitment means customers will pay for the value they receive. Getting back to the bakery department: yes, the end user is the consumer (grocery shopper) who desires fresh and delicious rolls and bread. Yes, they are willing to pay a premium for the availability of this brand. Not a bad reputation to have following you around. But it is the collective execution of departmental missions, such as the bakery department, that achieves these results. Their vigilance and discipline to assess their inputs (e.g., efficient ovens, excellent ingredients, and spectacular recipes) entering into their own departmental value chain and then transforming these inputs to the outputs of the timely delivery of fresh and quality rolls and bread to shipping, as well as eliminating waste, fulfills their internal mission. When a company is driven by an internal obsession to break down the walls to meet both internal and external customer expectations/requirements, it is deliberately controlling its own destiny more effectively and efficiently than its competitors do. The commitment to long-term, sustainable quality is now embodied by the nondefensive mantra, "You are only as good as your weakest value chain link." Quality begets quality.

Consequently, value chain optimization is fortified by departmental missions. The opportunity to meaningfully align team members' emotional commitments, strengths, and personal value propositions to the departmental mission will now be expanded by component number nine. Empowerment, here we come.

9. INDIVIDUAL OBJECTIVES/MANAGEMENT PERFORMANCE SYSTEM

Now that clear role definitions are formally developed for the departments with a uniform template, and are understood by the team, including key performance indicators and improvement objectives per member, it is time to assess the current management performance system and/or introduce a new and more responsive management by objective (MBO) process. Deloitte, in a 2016 public survey, found that "more than half the executives questioned (58 percent) believe that their current performance management approach drives neither employee engagement nor high performance."[28]

One such process—the work, planning, and review (WPR) system—does not confuse the annual performance review, which has been proven to discourage authentic feedback, with weighing one's annual compensation. Bruce Gibb, my coach, introduced me to the WPR system (which was created and named by GE in the 1960s) when I was building my own company in the early eighties, which, soon after my introduction to WPR, became Nasdaq listed. In a WPR system, mutual objective-setting and progress/performance review discussions take place more often than annually.

Personal development is the keystone to this process. A coaching style that establishes norms of trust, openness, and collaboration affirms the strengths of the employees and their commitment to the mission and to quality work. My company developed our WPR system from established practices. Today, I make this management performance system readily available to my clients. I have found that the following questions, when posed by a manager who is qualified and trained to utilize the WPR system, are the nucleus of an effective performance management system.

Questions from manager to subordinate

- What can I do as your manager to make your job easier?
- What am I doing and/or not doing to be effective in my role?
- Do you have any recommendations to improve what we do or how we do it?

On the flip side . . .

Questions to be answered by subordinate and shared with manager

- What am I doing that I should keep doing?
- What am I doing that I should change?

Mutual accountability and respect—or being in sync—can then take hold between the manger and subordinate in this vital linchpin. Both will realize that they are in this together for the greater good of the organization; that both are citizens of something bigger than their own individual roles and needs.

The Importance of Accurately Defined Individual Roles

I cannot overstate how vital accurate individual role definitions are to the high performance and job satisfaction of organizational members. A performance management system wanes in value without them. To make a point: Say, for instance, your first-tier (C-suite) and second-tier payroll is $300,000 per month. The absence of clear, relevant, and purposeful role definitions, underpinning a responsive management system, is costing you $60,000 per month on average (which is conservative) in lost productivity. But optimizing these two tiers of payroll expenditure with accurate and meaningful organization-wide roles will capture a significantly higher ROI on this monthly cash outlay. This does not need to be complicated. As stated by Jennifer Garvey Berger and Catherine Fitzgerald in their book, *Executive Coaching*, "The match between an executive's complexity of mind and the requirements of her/his role is critical for both effectiveness and job satisfaction. A role will be a poor match when it requires an order (level) that is higher or lower than the executive's capability."[29]

I will simplify this discussion with a "role fit" framework beginning with the CEO, C-suite, and next level of management. All roles fall into one of the following categories.

1. **There is a role fit:** The individual has the required capabilities and motivation for this position. The complexity (i.e., critical thinking skills, problem-solving capacity, emotional intelligence) of the role is matched with the environment demands (i.e., span of control, complex product and service offering, multiple and diverse stakeholder relationships). The employee is meeting or exceeding performance expectations. Job satisfaction (happiness factor) is high. Continued coaching and/or helpfulness are readily available for the subordinate. All parties contribute. Affirmation is given, beginning at the top. The organization-wide principles

of empowerment and accountability are further embedded into the culture.

2. **There is not a role fit because of overqualification:** The individual is overqualified for his or her position. This person has greater skills and/or motivation for the demands/requirements of this role. As a result, job satisfaction is low. The manager/supervisor should speedily ascertain what the subordinate's role aspirations are and optimize his/her contribution. Left unattended, the enterprise may lose a valuable member, diminishing the credibility of the manager/supervisor and impacting morale.

3. **There is not a role fit because of underqualification:** The individual is not qualified (in over their head) for his or her position. The employee is not achieving performance expectations. The person is lacking critical capabilities and/or motivation. The manager/supervisor may be in over their head as well. Job satisfaction is low; maybe for both parties. Critical coaching skills are required to address the nonperformance and possible accountability issues, beginning with the manager/supervisor. If this issue is not addressed, the espoused values of the organization are inconsistent, causing credibility and morale problems.

Let's move to application time. What role category do you fall into? Is it a cross between two? Or maybe a smattering of all three? Now, we are into some serious soul searching, beginning with you. Assessing the defined critical responsibilities in your role definition, which ones should be addressed to further optimize your role? In other words, what are the capabilities and/or motivation that you need to skill up on or further leverage/utilize?

I was recently coaching an owner and president (and control freak) who finally admitted, by realizing his own limitations, that his job satisfaction was negligible. He was miserable and angry. But more telling was his conclusion that he was in over his head and disdained management tasks and responsibilities. He'd been faking it for a long time in his present role. I sensed not only a relief on his part but also a measure of humility. Remember: the things you do to protect your ego/self-image may very well be the undoing of your own company.

Assess yourself in your role using the **Leadership Development Questionnaire,** Appendix item 3. Now move around your C-suite table and do the same assessment with your team members. Ask them to go through the exercise and then compare notes. Then you can go on (in another session) to Appendix item 5, a role analysis worksheet, titled **Role Definition Development,** that can strongly assist in this role-development process. Have each manager do the same for their own teams and then share the results with you. This exercise is concise and reveals loads of timely information. It is the foundation of a performance management and reward system, which is modeled at the top of the enterprise.

The corporate and departmental missions will have far more purpose and meaning, which will lead to emotional commitment from each employee. Why not root such a performance-enhancing system within your own enterprise's culture? A consistent management performance practice underpinned with accurate role definitions will enhance employee engagement and become a significant driver of an integrated culture.

10. INTEGRATED CULTURE

An integrated culture is the organization-wide process of embedding, managing, and aligning the stated core values, supporting norms, strategic vision, and mission. In a well-integrated culture, the cultural subsystems underlying departmental mission statements are consciously, conscientiously, and consistently supporting the current corporate strategy, mission, and goals. The extended value chain is self-managed and pridefully understood to be a foundation of the enterprise's competitive advantage and business strategy. The organization structure is optimal, anchored by clearly defined roles, yet still contingent upon the demand tasks of the external environment. Performance management, sustained by accurate goal setting, is viewed as an opportunity to be empowered and personally developed. Compensation and rewards are now more clearly tied to defined roles supporting departmental missions. The CEO's leadership/management style is in tune (readily adaptable) with the realities of the internal culture and the demands of the external environment. Team performance is a direct reflection of their leadership and management effectiveness. The CEO is consciously managing the polarities of leadership flexibility versus stability on one hand and environmental certainty versus uncertainty on the other.

In this strong, integrated culture, the leader encourages personal feedback in order to objectify what employees are experiencing and to be open (vulnerable) to what he or she does not see. Leadership adopts the **STP** gap analysis model, vigilantly assessing the current **S**tate, comprising the internal and external landscapes to make timely adaptive decisions, moving the organization to its **T**arget with a strategic business **P**lan. Deep integrity takes root in the culture. People are genuinely happy to work at their company. They care.

Leaders continuously gauge the temperature of their culture's climate (the working atmosphere), making sure it is not too hot (e.g., employees overwhelmed with work pace, impacting quality of service) or too cold (e.g., employees disengaged and emotionally alienated due to lack of information and poor communication)—working against the attainment of the strategic vision. The ideal temperature is evidenced: Current business practices and individual responsibilities are clear and reinforced by the stated values and a fair and equitable reward system; mission execution is dedicated; members are consistently engaged; there is flexibility; individual and organizational results are expected; emotional commitment is apparent.

Daniel Goleman concludes in his seminal *Harvard Business Review* article, "Leadership That Gets Results," that "We looked at the impact of climate on financial results—such as return on sales, revenue growth, efficiency, and profitability, [and] we found a direct correlation between the two. Leaders who used styles that positively affected the climate had decidedly better financial results than those who did not. That is not to say that organizational climate is the only driver of performance. Economic conditions and competitive dynamics matter enormously. But our analysis strongly suggests that climate accounts for nearly a third of results. And that's simply too much of an impact to ignore."[30]

There are a number of cultural assessment/survey instruments available, including the ones I've used with my clients. Most notably, the work of Terrence Deal has been particularly helpful. Also, I've utilized the Competing Values Framework of Robert Quinn and Kim Cameron for mergers and acquisitions and strategic alliances. Recently, as I've applied Alignment Strong, Daniel R. Denison's culture model/survey, integrating four cultural traits (mission, consistency, involvement, and adaptability), supported by twelve cultural indexes, has been very insightful and reassuring, supplying me with a framework and reference point on a pre- and post-engagement basis to categorize my observations. Denison's research is remarkably reliable and valid, linking culture to financial performance.

When my wife and I returned from Papua New Guinea, I was introduced to Dan Denison by my friend Bruce Gibb. Subsequently, Dan was kind enough to invite me to Ann Arbor, Michigan, to attend a culture survey certification workshop, which included room and meals, gratis. I was deeply impacted by the depth and breadth of their curriculum. Dan is an admirer of Edgar H. Schein, whose voluminous work on culture, leadership, and process consultation I studied in graduate school. Dan quotes Schein in one of his Denison Consulting publications: "Culture matters . . . If the organization begins to fail, this implies that elements of the culture have become dysfunctional and must change. Failure to understand culture and take it seriously can have disastrous consequences for an organization."[31]

In summary, the first nine understandings or **Integral Processes–Practices–Systems** explored so far in this chapter are Alignment Strong fully realized. The tenth component, the **Integrated Culture**, is a separately active element sustaining the alignment structure. The leader/chief alchemist is consciously orchestrating the alignment. He or she is standing, competitively postured, to discharge the integrating role effectively. Now one gets a glimpse of the potter's finished vase, the unique design, the balanced organization; accordingly, the total enterprise is aligned and postured in a leadership position to sustainably compete. Effective leadership is requested.

The CEO will masterfully choreograph Alignment Strong. Max De Pree, in his book *Leadership Is an Art*, declares that "Leadership is an art, something to be learned over time, not simply by reading books. Leadership is more tribal than scientific, more a weaving of relationships than an amassing of information, and, in that sense, I don't know how to pin it down in every detail."[32]

Masterfully choreographed, Alignment Strong will more than likely be applied in very muddled conditions. Keep in mind, as author James Joyce of *Finnegans Wake* fame wrote, "In the muddle is the sounddance."[33] Sounds evocative? I believe it is. In the disarrangement and untidiness of Alignment Strong's evolvement, dissonance diminishes, giving way to a synchro-meshing of all ten components. I betcha you would not pick this up in an MBA curriculum. The originality of this sound deeply resonates within yourself. You come to realize you have fashioned your own sounddance. Count on a developmental and embedding lag time of eighteen to twenty-four months to see meaningful and lasting results. Your change formula has been tested. As you transform your organization, morphing it "from what to what," remember that new beginnings eventually require complete endings, and this demands courage and endurance.

We have taken a significant excursion into the ten components constituting the Vitruvian organization. The plumb line should be clearly manifested in the discussion that I've led you through. Next you will find a hypothetical case study developed for you to see a clear and simple application of Alignment Strong. You may also, now or later, evaluate yourself/your organization utilizing the **Alignment Strong Assessment** that is Appendix item 1, at the end of this book.

A Case Study:
Without and With Alignment Strong

One way to illustrate how Alignment Strong differs from previous change initiatives—and outcomes—is to take a hypothetical but typical business situation and play it out utilizing a case study. So let's do that.

Mary Harris was the CEO for The Smithson Company, the world's leading producer of high-end tennis rackets, and she was facing a crucial board meeting. Company sales as measured by units sold were declining, and revenues had been sustained over the last two years only by a marketing strategy of promotion initiatives, which increased prices across Smithson's already high-cost model line. Key employee turnover had become a problem. Employee morale was stale. Lean manufacturing processes had taken their toll.

Harris, who'd worked her way up through the company ranks, had become CEO just three months before the unit sales began to decline. Externally, the economy was expanding. In general, people were spending money on sports equipment. As the company's highest-ranking non-family member (and the first woman to rise to that level), she was feeling high job anxiety.

Analysts said that Smithson's most valuable asset was its brand/image/reputation for high-quality products, going back sixty years to the company's founding by tennis champion Rod Smithson. But tennis was not a growing sport, and young athletes didn't really know or care about who Rod Smithson was, in spite of superstars such as Serena Williams and Roger Federer's recent feats on the courts.

Harris's dilemma was twofold: She had been unable to think of any ways to improve the product line, and her readings in business literature about best planning methods to apply in her company's situation were all over the map. Her go-to professional experts, including respected consultants, had offered remedies but not an overarching and integrated change framework. She knew the board had promoted her as someone with fresh ideas and energy, but she had more dread than confidence about the board meeting that would take place in a few days.

Case Outcome Without Alignment Strong

What was happening in Harris's company was a mix of well-founded impulses, traditions, and existing business practices and processes working at cross-purposes.

Tennis is a sports culture not known for abrupt changes. So in this scenario Harris decided not to employ a balanced framework such as Alignment Strong. Instead, the family owners and their longtime board representatives kept the focus on product quality, brand image, and athletic tradition.

The head of sales and marketing took cues and expectations from the family and board. The exclusivity of Smithson rackets was valued more than broadening the market in less affluent areas. Introducing medium-priced models was considered tantamount to diluting the brand.

The manufacturing side, proud of its quality work and materials, resisted the cost-cutting that the finance department put forth as prudent, bordering on risk-averse.

Heads of all the departments cited their pet examples of other companies that foundered because they went against one or more of the traditional Smithson values. Harris's leadership style as CEO, her decision-making effectiveness, and her conflict-resolution skills safely mirrored the founder and board's values.

New hires soon realized that being risk-averse was the way to be favored in job status. Loyalty was prized over candid conversation and empowerment. Cultural realities began to take hold. The core values of the organization began to manifest themselves in unhealthy behaviors (e.g., win-lose activities between departments, mistrust between managers and subordinates, putting self-interests before the welfare of the larger organization). And, not coincidentally, Smithson's weakening financial performance brought into question the organization's future sustainability.

With Alignment Strong

Late one night, just thirty-five hours before her board meeting was to begin, Harris received an email from a friend who had seen an advance copy of *Alignment Strong* and had attached it. Her friend was a partner in an established boutique investment banking firm and had graduated from the same university as Harris with an MBA. Harris valued her friend's background and past advice, and her intellectual curiosity spiked. She immediately scrutinized the Da Vinci schematic. She then plunged into reading the manuscript.

At 9:08 a.m. a day-and-a-half later, when Board Chairman Emerson Smithson looked her way and asked, "Any thoughts, Mary?" she was ready.

"I'd like to give you a very quick outline of a fresh approach. I'll just run through the highlights and hope we can then discuss them," she said.

These were the highlights.

1. The **core values statement** of The Smithson Company, though highly appreciated, focused only on high-quality tennis rackets. Harris pointed out that this statement should be expanded to

reflect the culture and the external marketplace. What was really core was not so much the tennis aspect, but the "high quality." That core value must be channeled and applied toward achieving a particular excellence in a broader mission of products and services. The company would include this value along with other, yet to be identified and defined, core values.

2. A new, five-year **strategic vision** was in order and would serve to drive coherency and alignment into the company culture. "Everyone in the company, from the top down," Harris explained, "will experience a sense of excitement and audacity." Rod Smithson's strategic vision was to form a thriving company that could sustain his core values. Though tradition became valuable, the brand was relevant in the market because the products were desirable at and beyond the moment of purchase.

3. The company ought to assess its **current mission**, define and prioritize its products and services, and examine its current **value proposition/competitive advantage**. Harris pointed out that "The Smithson Company should be open-minded to finding and keeping new customers, in ways that build on the company's glorious past and retain the sense of exclusivity with a premium price."

4. Of course, adaptability to these changes needed to be embodied from the top of the organization, Harris said, beginning with members in the room—including her—and all the way through to the newest hire and the longest-serving employee. "My **leadership style** must adapt to what this culture requires and the realities of the marketplace. Also, my decision-making effectiveness is worthy of assessment. I am willing to take my ego out of this process beginning with the assessment and development of my **team**. This process begins with myself. I will have a new

role definition and **template** for your review within thirty days, including a proven team-building development process. My executive team will then utilize the new role-definition template."

5. Harris suggested drafting a new and relevant **strategy/strategic narrative** for the next one to two years, with quarterly and annual considerations of revisions. "This will give us assurance that a broader strategic framework is in place so that we know what we are doing, why we are doing it, how we are doing it, and where we are going with it. Baked into this is a deliberate, as well as emergent, mindset. We intend to cross the river, yet we are prepared to reverse course, even in midstream."

6. Once the company had formalized its stated core values, strategic vision, mission and strategy narrative, it needed to formulate **specific, highly attainable, and time-lined goals**. Harris stressed, "This will be a fundamental component of building an effective team and will waterfall into the departments. Accountability will increase as a result of clear role expectations and goals."

7. Harris recommended taking a long look at The Smithson Company's present **organization structure** and examining its adaptability, customer responsiveness, effectiveness, and efficiency toward achieving the new goals. "I already expect to shift to a more agile and flexible structure with staff positions, combined with a more stable and predictable manufacturing structure. We will find our sweet spot between the two structures."

8. The company then needed to take a look at the organization horizontally—the internal **value chain**—to make sure all departments and functions had developed **mission statements**, including defined outputs/deliverables that would be aligned to and support the corporate mission and competitive advantage. Harris

noted, "Our internal value chain will be the source of operational excellence and the foundation of our competitive advantage."

9. In accord with steps 1 through 8, Harris proposed that the company develop an interactive/collaborative **management performance/reward system**, aligning **individual objectives/ personal strengths** to the strategy and goals of the company. "I've already researched a new system, which encourages more frequent coaching sessions, compared to our traditional annual performance review process."

10. As CEO, Harris said she was emotionally committed to lead the charge into the future, building a **high-performing executive team** that would reflect her commitment. "Admittedly, even with an MBA in hand and fifteen years of The Smithson Way, I am more convinced than ever that culture does eat strategy for breakfast. Research has verified that a strongly aligned organizational culture will outcompete a culturally misaligned organization. The resultant **integrated culture** of our company, what we will look and act like, both inside and outside, will be difficult for our rivals to replicate."

Case Outcome with Alignment Strong

In the conference room that day, after substantial discussion that was not without its awkward moments, occasional misunderstandings, stretches of unspoken stress, and various hesitations, the board came to the consensus that the company would utilize the framework and follow the path Harris had outlined, expressing their confidence in her. But what moved them off the dime?

One could guess that the pain of their current state was greater than the fear of the future. Or the risk of staying the same and doing nothing was outweighed by stepping into the future and adopting a new "planning" framework. Nevertheless, there was a supportive and affirming response. One may conclude that none of the board had ever seen a holistic and encompassing framework like Alignment Strong before. By habit, many decision makers (e.g., directors) move to the trees, and generate short-term solutions from a limited and possibly myopic perspective (elephant bites) without giving much thought to the forest (elephant), which expands a perspective and generates longer-term and more systemic solutions. The leader needs to do both at the same time.

Harris conjectured and concluded that a shift had taken place in her and their viewpoints, whether the board realized it or not. Change works that way, sometimes being nearly imperceptible. The Da Vinci Organizational Code brings things into balance. It is now Harris's and the board's reference point. Time to align.

Within three years, through these change initiatives and analyses from top to bottom, The Smithson Company became the highly regarded producer of not only tennis rackets but also top-quality pickle-ball paddles and lacrosse sticks and gloves, and—under a new brand—a specialized computer mouse for hard-core video gamers. With substantial new revenue and profits from these fast-growing sports and games, the Smithson work experience had become a result of integrated core values (quality traditions), strategy, mission, structure, intelligent risk-taking, disciplined processes, workplace respect, and high rewards. This strongly aligned culture was competitively postured to give its less-than-aligned rivals a run for their money, as well as attract and retain long-term employees and customers.

Building Effective Relationships

On occasion, I have been asked such things as, "What has not turned out the way you thought it would? As a change agent, what failures can you share? What was the most significant learning and forward application from your failures? Is there any one driving and recurring theme in your disappointments?"

Over thirty years, this work could have been fraught with unsuccessful change initiatives, but it wasn't. For the most part, my clients and I have been fortunate. I do have a few memorable accountings or case studies of failures and disappointments. However, I have attempted to be square with myself and with my clients. If I wasn't, I learned to own my own culpability (i.e., learning biases, emotional intelligence incompetence, personal blind spots, etc.). Certainly, I do not want to add fiction to a nonfiction book.

As previously noted, I have been a work in process as well. Personal development, splendid therapy, and coaching was required. I had to put skin into the game. I am as human as you, including my blind spots and hidden and unknown areas. But my theories were researched. I remained current in my academic field. My knowledge included business concepts and practices. I completed my tasks with clients on time and was well prepared. I was punctual and expected my client to be as invested in the work as I was. Mutual accountability to tasks/objectives was imperative on both sides. I sought authentic feedback and gave the same to my clients. A documented engagement/contract was put in place. If things did not mutually work out, with courtesy, either party could end the engagement with a handshake.

The takeaway, meta theme, or learning for me as a coach, co-founder, board chairman, and CEO of a publicly traded company, and a Papua New Guinea rainforest entrepreneur, is the vital ability to build sustainable, trusting relationships. Without that capability (interpersonal skills) and capacity (fortitude), whatever your mission may be, you will not achieve your optimal vision.

Building effective, interdependent relationships is critical for strong organizational alignment. Interdependency is the key assumption. It is required to create high-performance teams to achieve your stated goals. If interdependency is not a requirement, don't waste the time, effort, and expense to build such relationships, including teams. If it is a requirement, establish the rationale followed by clear expectations and objectives before the investment is made.

Applying a sports analogy, a game of golf requires little team interdependency compared to the complex, interdependent transition game of a basketball team. Where does your team fall on the interdependency continuum? Does your group have the characteristics of a hockey, football, or baseball team—perhaps somewhere between the polarities of a golf team and a basketball team? Have you rationalized and convinced yourself how essential interdependent and trusting relationships are to your organization? If so, are you emotionally committed to build such relationships, beginning with your own team?

Years ago, I was introduced to and professionally adopted a transactional-interactive relationship model as a tool to help my clients (and myself!) enhance relationships. It's called the Johari Window (JW) and was developed by psychologists Joseph Luft and Harrington Ingham ("Johari" comes from combining the beginnings of their first names). The JW is a handy and succinctly powerful framework to make sense out of one's interactions and relationships. It has been described as a model for mapping personality awareness—and for CEOs in particular, being forewarned is being forearmed. This insightful tool helps forewarn a CEO that he or she must sift through and filter critical relationships with stakeholders (e.g., C-suite team members, employees, strategic alliances, board members, suppliers, customers, competitors) to gain discernment. This means that you get smarter, quicker, and also more deliberate. It forearms you, by helping you become more astute in making commitments.

The Johari Window is made up of four interrelated windowpanes. In order to understand each area, one must comprehend the other three areas.

THE JOHARI WINDOW

OPEN
Things we know about ourselves and others know about us.

BLIND
Things others know about us that we do not know.

HIDDEN
Things we know about ourselves that others do not know.

UNKNOWN
Things neither we nor others know about us.

The Johari Window is a tool to make sense of interactions and relationships—
yours as well as those of individuals you work with.

All human relationships are based on things we know and do not know about ourselves and about others. Applying this to interconnections, there are four areas, as described by the JW's authors, that influence all of our relationships. I refer to these areas as windowpanes, which together form the larger Johari Window. The four areas depicted in the Johari Window illustration are labeled as "the open," "the hidden," "the blind," and "the unknown."

These four windowpanes are interrelated. In order to understand each area, you must comprehend the other three. Internet-available formats of the JW to illustrate its application are a keyboard away. The preceding figure presents a helpful JW schematic. This, along with a comprehensive explanation, was originally published by Salenger Educational Media in a JW leadership guide, "As Others See Us: A Look at Interpersonal Relationships."[1] I have incorporated their simple but very precise insights into this framework.

The Four Windowpanes

1. **The open area:** This is the aspect of a person that is public. It is common knowledge and information that is readily available or easily accessible (e.g., one's name, title, position, resume, age, events, fame, history, legacy, achievements, failures). We can fool ourselves into believing everything that is made public. That's because there's a sucker born every minute. Yet the expansion of one's open/public area or windowpane is a high-minded goal that comes with integrity. To expose oneself to the open area by revealing your hidden area or acknowledging your blind spots is an act of vulnerability. In today's social media landscape, attentiveness is warranted amid the crazed, superficial, manic drive to supply information or to ingest information. Egos are immensely inflated, whether it is the sender of the information or the receiver of the information. There is a lot of gamesmanship in the open area. In its

zeal to supply information, today's social media fuels this area's expansion. Authenticity wanes, as it is veneered by superficiality. One may be quickly punished for naiveté by assuming and/or trusting haphazardly.

Yet the expansion of this windowpane is the worthy goal of an authentic, interdependent relationship; the hidden and blind areas have been reduced because of people's willingness to be vulnerable. On a more satirical and cautious note, the musician Van Morrison underscored the incessant nature and shallowness of outward appearances and called it the "name game," which all of us get caught up in at one time or another. In his song "New Biography" from the album *Back on Top*, Morrison sings about how no one can truly know him unless they know his history. There has to be some truth to knowing someone, being vulnerable to their "pain," before you can truly claim to know them well. And isn't that true for all of us? We must delve under the surface. The leader has the vital responsibility to assess critical stakeholder relationships in order to be self- and socially aware of what is going on in relationships. Reducing the gamesmanship Van Morrison refers to will certainly help. If you don't have awareness skills that comprise social, political, and self, there is a strong possibility you may end up with smoke and mirrors in the open area. (The next section, Johari Window Application: A Live Wire, describes a personal example of smoke and mirrors.)

2. The hidden area: This windowpane represents all the things we know about ourselves that we choose to keep private. We build clever personas, masks, and fortresses to keep secret what we believe will hurt or diminish ourselves (e.g., weaknesses, unused strengths, shameful events, wounds, failures, talents, inadequacies). A professor in graduate school referred to our more unsavory attributes as "core rot." It belongs in this windowpane. For many CEOs, the fear of failure is nicely concealed in this windowpane. One takes great strides to be invulnerable. Talkers—those skilled in monologues, the controllers of conversation—are often experts in avoiding self-disclosure. The cloistered cave dwellers of insularity are clever. At the end of an evening, you realize you don't know one damn thing about that person. Yet they know a lot about you. Am I being paranoid? It has been claimed that "paranoia can link up with reality now and then."[2]

On the other hand, for the more curious risk-takers, a two-way interaction, where there is a free-flow sharing of the hidden areas, may be edifying and refreshing, absent emotional vomit (emotional and theatrical drama) that only reinforces invulnerability, keeping the hidden area intact. Nonetheless, conviction, discernment, and empathy are sound attributes in the effort to reduce the size of this area. Ralph Waldo Emerson once commented, "I would walk a hundred miles in a snowstorm to have a good conversation." Such a conversation may involve revealing your hidden area in your role as the leader of your own team. As of late, have you walked a hundred miles in a snowstorm to have a good conversation? Recently, two department heads in one company, separated by ten feet, concluded, after six months, that it might be a good idea to stop texting and have a one-on-one conversation pertaining to communication issues and conflicts between their departments. It was not a hundred miles, but the effort to leave their work stations and walk ten feet to have a good conversation was a significant breakthrough.

3. The blind area: Problematically, this windowpane is obtrusive by nature. It is what others see in you that you do not see in yourself—or don't welcome seeing in yourself—whether it's strengths or weaknesses (e.g., intelligence, lack of confidence, beauty, destructive habits, unused strengths, narcissism, empathy, bullying). Outside of the C-suite, members of the organization will grow alarmed when they perceive that the top of the company is in collective denial. The emperor is walking around butt naked. For an enterprise, collective blind spots in the C-suite can spell disaster inside the company and in the marketplace.

In their 2018 book, *What Are Your Blind Spots? Conquering the 5 Misconceptions that Hold Leaders Back,* authors Jim Haudan and Rich Berens identify leadership blind spots in the areas of purpose, story, engagement, trust, and truth. Unfettered, these blind spots are destructive forces working against an Alignment Strong enterprise and a competitive leadership posture. The two change practitioners conclude that "many leaders' long-held and no longer relevant beliefs regarding human nature in the workplace" operate against engaging the organization, diminish performance, and weaken competitive leadership posture. Citing research, the authors share, "We know that 60 to 90 percent of all strategies are not executed, 70 percent of people in organizations are not actively engaged, and annually, more than a half a trillion dollars' worth of economic value is not realized in the United States alone as a result."[3]

All human beings have a set of filters called subjectivity. But very few people realize these filters define one's reality. You and your filters are the same. You can't see them, but others do. Author Daniel Goleman of *Emotional Intelligence* fame calls this conundrum "the CEO disease,"[4] the vital lies we *all* tell ourselves in order to keep the Superman costume from being peeled off with the truth. Consequently, team members fear telling their boss and peers the truth, therefore leaving leadership and colleagues untouched by what they need to hear.

Listening skills are jaded by select memory—a well-conditioned filter system that is another indicator of a person who is unwilling to hear the feedback. This is a tiresome and well-rehearsed defensive routine. You might get frustrated with that person and conclude, "They never really get it." What message does this unwillingness to listen give to the organization? Possibly, the fact that loyalty to maintain the status quo is more valued than telling the truth. If such is the case, organization-wide empowerment is weakened.

Take some time to examine the core values of loyalty and truth. Which one is more prized in your organization today? Why? How does leadership exemplify these values to its members? These are thought-provoking and sobering questions. Take the time to answer them with your team. David L. Dotlich and Peter C. Cairo's book *Why CEOs Fail* characterizes the twelve derailers (dysfunctional attributes) or personal blind spots that bring CEOs down. It is a required read for my clients because when a leader can recognize their own—and others'—blind spots, they become infinitely more effective as a leader; one who can more successfully build and maintain effective relationships and teams. If they don't identify their own blind spots and do something about them, the authors conclude, the CEO will fail.

From an affirmative perspective, once a CEO is able to access their own or another person's blind spot, they should prize this exquisite gift. *The Man Who Listens to Horses*, a book written by horse whisperer Monty Roberts, makes the point: "I allowed him back, soothed him and talked to him, and gave him a good stroke between the eyes. It is not essential to use the area between the eyes as the stroking point, but it seems to be more effective to touch the horse here than any other part of the body. There is general consensus that for a horse to let you into a part of the anatomy that he cannot see is the ultimate expression of trust."[5]

The CEO becomes a "horse whisperer," not working with horses of course, but with important and complex relationships. A leader, deftly, with patience and gentleness, draws out an individual by touching on a vulnerable area that the person cannot see themselves. By permitting the CEO to do this, the other individual bestows the ultimate expression of trust. As a coach, this is a very honorable and sacred part of my practice. The author Henri J. M. Nouwen wrote, "What is most intimate is also what frightens us the most."[6]

4. The unknown area: Mystery and intrigue distinguish this windowpane. This area is unknown to ourselves as well as to others. It takes a CEO with exceptional courage to discover what he or she does not know—about himself or herself, team members, the enterprise, and the marketplace. Admitting "I don't know" is an act of vulnerability. But the act in itself permits one to explore with others what is in the future—accessing the unknown, including personal hopes and fears. By consciously focusing on building effective relationships, the CEO can lead team members to share their hidden areas and be open to examining their blind areas. If the leader declines this responsibility, then invulnerability, accompanied by stoicism and emotionless interactions, will possibly resonate among employees. These attitudes will go viral within the company, negatively impacting the culture.

Some of the most significant C-suite team building I have observed is when members explore the unknown together by exposing hidden areas and being open to examine one another's blind spots. I have included a **Team Development Exercise Module** as Appendix item 6. Since the mid-nineties, the significant work of Daniel Goleman's *Emotional Intelligence* has positively influenced my executive coaching practice. The Team Development Module integrates Goleman's EI competencies with the Johari Window of Luft and Ingham. With its combination of tools, this module will instruct you on how to increase role effectiveness in the C-suite as well as to build a higher-performing team.

Again, it is indispensable that the leader demonstrates the willingness and courage to move into the unknown. Vulnerability, openness to inquiry, and engagement—underscored by humbleness—are good foundations when you find yourself in the dark, in a maze, or struggling with unimaginable, complex, and novel problems and challenges. The act of approachability and nondefensiveness will reduce uncertainty in the C-suite, with organization members, customers, and other critical stakeholders. Nevertheless, the CEO is obliged to execute his or her strategizing and missioning responsibilities in order to move the organization into the future and this windowpane labeled as the unknown area.

Deliberate interactions to reduce, diminish, pierce, and enter the hidden, blind, and unknown areas will ultimately expand the open area, resulting in more transparent, authentic, and trusting relationships.

Johari Window Application: A Live Wire

I want to share a personal experience embodying the JW. One day, I received a phone call from a turnaround firm and was informed that their client (a bank) wanted a manufacturing company to take proactive measures to stem a persistent, negative cash flow problem.

The manufacturing company's top-line revenue was not the issue. Bottom-line results were not meeting profitability expectations in light of the bank loan covenants. Gross profit margins were significantly poor and machine inventory was at a high level. The servicing department was stretched due to poor machine design, and production was blaming engineering. The marketing and sales department was deflated due to a loss of confidence in their own products and services. The bank was concerned, but even more alarming was the company's customers' dependency on a vital supply of custom machinery and servicing in a highly competitive market.

The turnaround firm proposed an engagement with my firm. I interpreted that this opportunity would be a soft engagement (consultative/collaborative approach) versus a hard engagement where an interim CEO is put into place (direct/coercive approach). That should have been a warning sign for me. Usually the "soft" issues are the "hard" issues. I was captivated by the challenge. Bravado and a sense of heroism emboldened me to meet with the CEO of the manufacturing company.

A few days later, the chiseled, finely attired owner/CEO of the manufacturing company bought me a martini at the bar in the Detroit Athletic Club (network bastion of Detroit). This rite of passage led to an exquisite dinner. We exchanged perfunctory inquiries. He concluded we should work together and asked me to please send him an engagement letter. It was that simple and that quick.

The open area was a high-speed shutter. I was impressed by his academic pedigree, current business and social networks, and positional power invested in his sole ownership and title. *Presto.* In my enthusiasm, I'd had little time to probe the hidden area, explore for any blind spots, or wonder if he had any idea of why he had the cash flow problem that the bank claimed existed. Also, without an afterthought, I'd assumed he'd been transparent and had been to the unknown and back with loads of insights and applications. I sorely paid for my presumptuousness as I entered into this engagement.

Once I was introduced to the executive team, I then moved into an organizational assessment, utilizing interviews, surveys, and workplace observations by roaming around and chatting with employees.

I soon concluded a silo (territorial) mentality existed, evidenced by a lack of cooperation between departments. Win-lose or lose-lose attitudes predominated, versus a win-win attitude. More concerning for the employees was a fear and uncertainty of the future. They thought the company was out of sync. Symptomatically, leadership was neither seen nor felt throughout the company. I spent little time with the CEO, and he assured me that his company's problems were outside of his C-suite. I could not crack the code.

In conversation after conversation, and meeting after meeting, people were not willing to criticize the boss but were willing to examine their own deficiencies and blind spots in an attempt to fix their own departmental issues as well as bridge the silos, claiming that was where the problems were. I was blind to something. The culture had been enveloped by anxiety. Apprehensiveness was in high gear. Where was the fountainhead?

I could not put my finger on the problem until I decided to consciously probe with one department head. I was determined to create enough empathy and trust to surface what was really going on. It takes a great deal of effort to have another person become vulnerable enough to share their hidden area. The department head fully disclosed she was entangled in an extramarital affair with the CEO, but the CEO didn't know that everyone in management knew about the affair. "My oh my," I mused as I drove home late that afternoon, "nothing surprises me anymore. How in the hell did I get myself into this double bind?" Opining on this dilemma, I realized it was time for the consultant to apply his skills to himself.

As I stepped out of the fishbowl, reflecting on my experience, I soon realized I was in another experience of reflection on the situation. This reflection drove clarity into my own relationship with the CEO. I recounted writer and philosopher Aldous Huxley's admonition, "Experience is not what happens to you, it's what you do with what happens to you."[7] Serious pondering helped me deduce that I would terminate the engagement, suggesting the CEO should have a talk with the turnaround firm and make decisions/amends to satisfy the bank, in an attempt to turn his company around. Unfortunately, he needed to go first to his own credibility bank in order to save himself. It seemed to have run out of funds. Smote, I felt guilt by association, but there was no way I could lead any attempt to repair the damage. Accordingly, a competitor acquired the company. Soon after I disengaged, and after self-reflection, meaningful insights crystallized for myself; wisdom percolated and rose to the surface.

The JW configuration that follows illustrates—by the relative sizes of the windows—my first and last encounters with the CEO as I now reflect on this experience. The sensing meeting was characterized by verbosity in a small open area that bordered on cosmetic. The omission of any personal culpability for the company's problems created the inordinate size of the hidden area. Consequently, the non-probed blind area was a lapse and failure on my part and kept this windowpane static. The unknown area was largely ignored but inflated. I wrongly assumed that an integrated strategic vision was intact at the top of the organization. I relied on company literature, nice-sounding values, mission and vision mantras/statements displayed on the walls of the C-suite, and a shallow organizational/cultural assessment. Without surprise, by utilizing the JW windowpanes, the departing configuration for this relationship is now depicted.

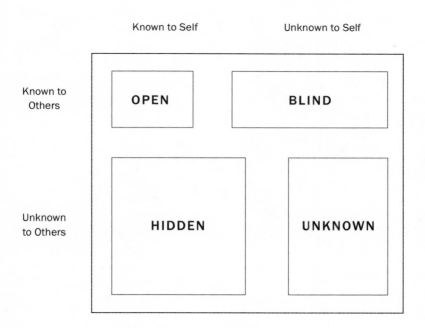

The relative size of each pane of a Johari Window
indicates the importance of its contents.

Once more, the deliberate interactions to disclose the hidden, pierce the blind, and enter into the unknown areas will ultimately expand the open area, resulting in more transparent, authentic, and trusting relationships. The benefits of expanding the open area of the window are significant. I become more effective as a coach/consultant. The CEO would possibly have enhanced his role effectiveness. Maybe, employee engagement would have taken on a new and purposeful meaning, as members of the organization became more open and responsive to and with one another, resulting in a healthier and higher-performing culture. Without fanfare, I continue on the path of an agile learner. Through self-examination and self-trust, I continue to embrace a growth mindset as I master the panes of the Johari Window to build effective relationships. And so can you.

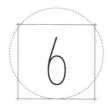

Symphony of the Synthesist

Just like in a symphony, where a composer puts notes together to create original music, so it is with my work presented in this book. In a symphony, every note the composer uses is already in existence, but it is the way the composer positions the notes together and synthesizes them into a harmonious piece that is unique.

Many of the ideas and knowledge I've presented may be familiar to you, but I trust that the way the ideas and knowledge are composed will spark a new appreciation, perspective, and understanding on how to incorporate what I call the Wisdom Life Chart into your own life. The music never ends. You can go on to create your own symphony.

The Wisdom Life Chart is essentially this:

Experience + Knowledge + Self Reflection = Wisdom

But take this into account: Before you can do the arithmetic of the Wisdom Life Chart accurately, you may need to accomplish some subtraction—a stripping away of self-delusion, fear, ego fortresses, allegiance to your personal past, unwillingness to examine your blind spots, and so on. You will need to become vulnerable to what is genuine. This requires courage. To evolve to a "no-face"—as described in the Preface—demands a willingness to contract your ego. Ouch! But I know of no other way to gain humility.

In my case, I had to become "transparent to the transcendent," in the words of the American thinker Joseph Campbell—a symphonic synthesizer himself who is among the authors I readily credit in the section titled "Wisdom's Invitation." When your internal compass is in place, and you can be square with yourself and others, the flywheel of self-acceptance and self-knowing kicks in. Deep integrity will take root within you. As a symphonist, practice will beget quality. You will become the composer. Your perspective is transcending. You will become the chairman of a more expansive and intricate board than you ever imagined. Besides your organization, your life is intricately influenced and enriched by your wisdom.

To achieve the full truth of what Campbell writes about, *self-reflection* must also be *social reflection*. For effectiveness, the sum of your introspection needs to play out in the auditorium of your society—your tribe or company or nonprofit; your community. And then you should be fully vulnerable to letting others play back or mirror the results of your effort. Quality composers know how good their music is, regardless of the audience and critics. They are grounded in themselves and do not fear mirrors. When you care for what is important, you will become infused with a new understanding of quality leadership. Care and quality go hand-in-hand in a grip that squeezes out self-fraudulence and fraudulence in relationships. Your emotional and cognitive empathy, with competences to comprehend and integrate how others feel and think, will ensure that you are building authentic trust. Again, this trust-building starts within you. Self-trust is a precious commodity, akin to fine silver and gold. You will become more valuable.

Now, as a synthesist I want to convey to you three vignettes, which contain all of the elements in the Wisdom Life Chart.

THE CAMPFIRE STRATEGY:
CREATING PSYCHOLOGICAL SAFETY

This particular experience is about recommending an effective developmental strategy to help leaders and their teams find vulnerability and trust. Earlier on in my practice, a young governor asked me to fly into his state capital to meet at his official mansion. He wanted to check me out—first, for chemistry, and second, to discuss a change framework for his state's health care system. I attended a lunch meeting that included select members of his cabinet, two family members, and a few advisors. The only person missing was his limousine driver, who effectively played the gatekeeper's role, by checking me out on the drive from the airport to the mansion. I concluded he was a member of the "kitchen cabinet."

After delicious barbecue in the formal dining room with his entourage, the governor warranted that there was "clickability" between us, and we huddled together, one-on-one in the library. This ambitious governor, also a Harvard MBA graduate, resonated vulnerability with his open-ended questions. Quickly, I surmised his statewide strategic vision for health care. We then moved to an assessment of what forces/factors were driving and contributing to his vision, and what forces/factors were restraining his vision. We both took notes. The discussion then moved to the plan: How would he get there? I referenced a strategic planning waterfall process (my then-named model of Alliance Strong, circa 1990). He comprehended the framework and asked, "What is the first step? How do I begin?"

My answer was flippant: "You need to have a 'campfire' with your cabinet members." Then I quickly explained that it was time to slow down and take a break from his immediate tasks (his day job). The brevity and simplicity stunned him. Imagining my own Cub Scout and Boy Scout campfire days, I could only guess what was going through his mind.

He got the metaphorical picture. Maybe he was a Cub or Boy Scout. I did not inquire. But he caught on that campfires, for the most part, slow people down and bring them together. Fervently, the governor responded, "Yes, and to do what?"

Caught up in his enthusiasm, I suggested he sequester his team to establish group norms and core values, share personal visions and individual cabinet member expectations, and then for him to impart his strategic vision. It was time to put some logs on a fire, get into a circle, have uninterrupted dialogue (suspend personal assumptions), and listen and respond with respect. This dialogue would discourage hidden agendas and would be underscored by transparency and a psychological contract that his team was in this together for the betterment of the state. I encouraged him to set a norm of truth before loyalty. It was a distinction he had never given much thought to. No harm would come to anyone for telling one another, and him, the truth. I wonder to this day, if a POTUS, from any party, would be this vulnerable. If he or she was, it might turn out to be one helluva cabinet/administration.

My self-awareness kicked in. I felt emboldened by his emotional reaction and body language. I affirmed him with my own enthusiasm and a sense of fusion with this stranger. By doing so, I crossed the line and jumped into his fishbowl by projecting my own values. Helpfulness and empathy exuded from me, a supposedly "objective clinical independent" third-party change agent. It is difficult for me to refrain from being subjective and being personal. Akin to a CEO struggling to balance long-term and short-term priorities, I struggle with the balance of subjectivity and objectivity, and seem to repeatedly and reflexively move into subjectivity. At times, I suffer the consequences of my own vulnerability and get wounded for my presumptuousness and impulsiveness. Have I crossed the line by over-personalizing? I've been told that change agents should expect to be misunderstood, and being a catalyst for change may be dangerous to your health; that we should keep professional distance and err on the side of being objective and more remote. Yet I continue to remain open and be personal and not downplay this embedded proclivity. I would rather err and overcompensate on being subjective. It is worth it. I find it deeply rewarding. It is a choice point and blind spot that I am aware of. Yet, I am determined to find a balance, to integrate objectivity and subjectivity. That is enough personal disclosure from my hidden area; time to get back to this experience.

Excitedly, the governor wanted me to generate what resulted in a forty-page request for proposal (RFP). Ultimately, continuing to work with the governor would have required me to move to his state to become the third-party change agent/catalyst. I respectfully declined, but the major takeaway for me and hopefully the governor was the crystallization of a "Campfire Strategy," the platform he could use to drive change, beginning with his cabinet and waterfalling into the state government. The health care system was now part of a bigger picture (system). If I impart anything to you in this book, it is the power of vulnerability, exemplified by the leader, resulting in the haven called psychological safety.

In the end, the hierarchy (cabinet) needs to be assembled, with roles defined, execution demanded, and results expected. But I knew the state government's imperative to serve citizens and to protect their welfare would not suffer by taking time-outs to have campfires. In a tribal tradition, both the campfire and the hunting party modes are essential. The hunting party—just like the cabinet/team—is obliged to fulfill the mission or the village goes hungry. But without the campfire mode as well, the mission is diluted and alignment will be a figment of your imagination. It will be without a collective soul.

Campfires connect people to one another, enabling members to further comprehend each other. Members are off executive alert to have the time to share stories, successes, failures, and visions with one another. They will soon move back into a hunting party mode. The campfire encourages us to expose our cracks, growing into a brighter and lighter fire.

THE ART FORM OF TEAM BUILDING:
HUMAN NATURE IS UNIVERSAL

Team building is an art form in the quest for Alignment Strong, whether the process is explicit—for example, "We are going to further study and apply Patrick Lencioni's 'Five Dysfunctions' team-building model and assess our group today"—or implicit, as in, "We are going to have an informal roundtable gathering and share what is going on in our company and what you are feeling and thinking about, working together as the leadership team." In this process, applying the Wisdom Life Chart, we learn about ourselves. We realize that not only are we an individual human system called ourselves (e.g., Vitruvian Man), but the team is a system; the organization is a system. It is all linked. There is an affinity. As human beings, we are connected by common motives and needs. By applying a worthy team-building process such as a Campfire Strategy, this connection is crystallized for both leaders and members. We can then comprehend our collective humanness and build trust at a deeper level and broader scope in relationships.

The execution of the mission is driven by survival. All human beings are wired to survive. We need the hunting party or we literally starve, whether it is food for the village or top-line revenue and positive cash flow for the company. The campfire creates the psychological setting to connect and move into the future—the unknown—together. Team members will practice and reinforce vulnerability. An ethos of self-forgiveness, empathy, and forgiveness of others emanates. Anne Rød and Marita Fridjhon summarize our common motives as human beings in their book, *Creating Intelligent Teams*. They state that "because the human brain is wired for survival, we can feel threatened and respond negatively when

- We are afraid of losing our status and relevance.
- We are afraid of not knowing and not being involved.

- We are afraid of losing control or influence.
- We are afraid of not belonging.
- We are afraid of not being treated with respect and empathy."[1]

Human nature is human nature. That is why the need for the Alignment Strong model is the same everywhere around the world—in developing and developed countries, whether in Australia or Latin America, China, Japan, or Russia, as purported by Kimberley Barker in the Foreword.

Having lived in a remote village as an American organizational development practitioner in Papua New Guinea, I can attest that these same applications hold true. There are no boundaries. Alignment Strong is needed throughout the world now more than ever, and across generations. My three daughters, who are in their mid-twenties, have exclaimed that this book is relevant to them today in their vocations. They have applied it in their jobs. Fortunately, all three of them are proactive and are empowered by their organizations. Kimberley Barker affirms that her students at the end of the graduate level would relate to Alignment Strong without exception and find enormous relevancy in the model.

Here's an example of the relevance of human nature in a team-building context. I designed and facilitated an off-site strategic planning retreat for a global logistics company, comprising fifty people, including the C-suite, six European agents, twenty domestic agents, various staff, and twelve department heads. The retreat's agenda was based on an annual organizational assessment and a current SWOT analysis. The first day concluded. Drinks and dinner followed. We all gathered at a bar, late in the evening, and "implicit team building" ensued. I soon surmised the agenda was not addressing the real systemic cultural issues. Gossiping, backbiting, dirty, rotten attitudes (DRAs), triangulating, and negativity dominated the conversation. The retreat was set on course to be purely cosmetic—a waste of time, effort, and money. These covert behaviors and informal processes, unwittingly or not, were making a sham of the retreat and the enterprise.

I sequestered the three owners in a suite and shared my observations. Chagrined, they implored, "What do we do?" I responded by asking them if they were willing to tear up the agenda, take down all of the posted flip chart pages on the walls, and create a circle of chairs to welcome the participants the next morning, to have an open discussion without time limits. I questioned the group, "What is really going on here?" It was time for all of the participants to reveal what was below the tip of the iceberg in their company and, hopefully, within themselves. Sheepishly, they agreed.

Anxiety—the healthy anxiety called creative tension—kicked in, and was pulling the owners to their vision. But there are no guarantees in leading change. If you are going to throw the grenade, you have to be willing to pull the pin. We would soon test the hypothesis: Would the risk of exposure and being vulnerable be worth uncertain rewards? All of us were about to find out.

The session began at 9 a.m. Fifty bewildered people sat in a circle and stared at one another, some with obvious hangovers. The CEO, his brother, and one other officer made opening comments. They explained what we were doing, why we were doing it, and how this would work. It was campfire time. Following their comments, I shared the question "What is really going on here?" and printed it on a flip chart. I felt like I was giving an invocation. The norms were set. Whoever wanted to speak was free to take the opportunity, provided everyone was committed to listening without judgment and defensiveness. The end goal was to better the organization, putting it before self-interest.

Silence reigned for the first five to ten minutes. Nervously, a woman gazed at the CEO and finally said, "For seventeen years you have treated me like crap. Never once have you ever acknowledged my commitment to your company. I question if I want to move forward with this firm."

Her eyes moistened, as did those of the CEO. Everyone witnessed the exchange of emotional empathy. This was an encouraging sign. One by one, members spoke up, expressing their needs to belong, to be respected, and to know they were relevant to one another and the organization. Openly, the organization-wide team members expressed deep motivations and convictions, which were then acknowledged by the owners and the C-suite, who received the feedback without defensiveness.

The harmonizing was a beautiful thing to witness. There was no malice. People were affirming one another's vulnerability. The team spiraled upward to a new place (a sense of community and unity) they had not collectively experienced before; they passed a significant highway marker. I was reminded of my rainforest CEO days in Papua New Guinea and the instruction and wisdom I received from the book *Spiral Dynamics*. Authors Don Beck and Christopher Cowan respectfully quote the adult human development theorist Clare Graves: "Damn it all, a person has the right to be who he is."[2]

This annual planning retreat was the catalyst for organization-wide team building. It was not planned. It just happened, resulting in a defined core values statement and supporting norms that would guide the company into its preferred future. A critical component of Alignment Strong fell into place. This shared-values process took six months from start to finish. The company never looked back. Connected hip to hip, they quadrupled top-line revenue and profits in seven years and were acquired by a European company. An economic value added (EVA) incentive system was put into place to financially reward management for their commitment and performance at the time of retirement and/or acquisition.

Ponder again the five motivators and make notations.

- Fear of losing our status and relevance
- Fear of not knowing and not being involved
- Fear of losing control or influence

- Fear of not belonging
- Fear of not being treated with respect and empathy

Which ones may be impacting members of your own team? Is one or more of these motivators challenging you? By being vulnerable, are you worried about losing control or influence with your team or board? What new skills and behaviors (e.g., having an accurate self-assessment by knowing your own strengths, deficiencies, listening and responding with empathy, being aware of your own emotions) can you envision in your ideal, effective role, keeping these motivators in mind? What would the script look like when you have a significant conversation with a key relationship? Stop now, and really reflect on what I've just challenged you to do. By taking the time to reflect and contemplate, you are literally taking emotional self-control of the impulse to speed up and read on. By slowing down, in the long run, you speed up. Practice is required. So, go back to the questions and engage yourself.

Having coached C-suites in many enterprises, I have found these motivators are not hard to spot once members are willing to open up and talk. Rehearse and envision the interaction or coaching steps before you engage. The results of effectively coaching your subordinates can be significant to the building of a high-performance team as well, provided you are willing to take the time to do it capably.

A sound developmental team model, such as Patrick Lencioni's *The Five Dysfunctions of a Team*, sequentially describes five breakthrough stages to building a result-focused team. Lencioni names the five dysfunctions: (1) Absence of Trust, (2) Fear of Conflict, (3) Lack of Commitment, (4) Avoidance of Accountability, and (5) Inattention to Results.[3] I was introduced to his book in 2002 and have applied his model to clients and villagers both in America and Papua New Guinea. I have seen self-trust and team trust displace invulnerability; fear of conflict penetrated; emotional commitment heightened; accountability standards raised to high levels, discouraging avoidance and encouraging peer vigilance; and attention to results, being focused on the endgame (achievement of strategic vison and execution of goals) versus egocentricity, driven by status and ego.

Team building is an art form. You are the symphonist. This is personal. Human nature is universal. We are all connected.

CULTURAL DNA: THE ENTERPRISE'S MINDSET

Unmistakably, fear of the unknown is the greatest deterrent to forward motion into the future to attain the enterprise's strategic vision. Yet it is the kiln for wisdom. Vulnerability is summoned, demonstrated by the CEO, and the team enters the unknown area with greater hope and confidence. Personal risk taking is exemplified. Again, a leader is charged with creating a "growth mindset" as opposed to a "fixed mindset." As Carol S. Dweck explains in *Mindset*, individuals with a fixed mindset are always on the move, with urgency, to repeatedly hold themselves in an unchangeable/uncompromising position, often perched above others, where they have to relentlessly demonstrate themselves. Errors or failure are unacceptable. In other words, you only have a limited amount of intelligence, personality/temperament, and moral attributes and are doomed to a path of constantly proving yourself by seeking validation. Dweck further explains that people with a growth mindset see errors, mistakes, and failures as windows of opportunities to learn and improve themselves: "The growth mindset is based on the belief that your basic qualities are things you can cultivate through your efforts. Although people may differ in their initial talents and aptitudes, interest, or temperaments—everyone can change and grow through application and experience."[4]

Years of practice and toil have brought me to an understanding that the organization's values and underlying assumptions form the embryo of any organizational mindset. The embryo is embedded at a deep level of an organization, akin to the depth of an iceberg. Even deeper are the underlying assumptions or DNA, which are ultimately replicated by the values and the norms—expected behaviors for the organization. For example, the value labeled "trust" is driven by a wholehearted assumption. Does the founder or a CEO believe trust is inherently implicit with an employee, customer, or supplier until that trust is broken, or does the founder or CEO implicitly mistrust these relationships at the onset, until the trust is explicitly earned? In this one value alone, this nuance has a powerful influence on the culture of the enterprise and its competitive posture, for better or worse, in the marketplace.

The mindset is the character of the enterprise. It all begins and ends with values. A growth mindset is fundamental to a culture of trust, characterized by agile learning, creating a willingness within a safe harbor to take risks. What a perfect antidote for groupthink. I consider such a mindset as an emanation of the organization's DNA that makes it possible for an enterprise to become Alignment Strong.

Consequently, a mindset invariably stems from the founders, owners, CEO, or an established leadership team. The external environment constantly challenges and tests this mindset. It would be foolish and dangerous for an organization not to be aware of the demands and tasks imposed on it by the ecosystem in which it competes and to which it must adapt.

In her book, Dweck assists the reader to distinguish the difference between the two mindsets by employing two variables: intelligence and personal qualities. The "intelligence variable comes into play when situations involve mental ability (e.g., facts, information, smartness, reasoning, braininess). The personal variable comes into play in situations that involve your personal qualities (e.g., attitude, character, disposition, engagement)."[5] Dweck further describes the personal variable: "For example, how dependable, cooperative, caring you are or socially skilled you are."[6] The fixed mindset makes you anxious about how you'll be judged. It is intelligence driven. The growth mindset motivates one to improvement. It is developmental, relational, and reinforces personal risk-taking.

The sets of statements and commentary from Dweck's book that follow reveal how subtle the differences are between the fixed and growth mindsets. Yet the growth mindset makes all the difference in the world for a leader in charge of influencing the culture of the company. This is the foundation for agile learning.

Set One (Intelligence Qualities)

1. Your intelligence is something very basic about you that you can't change very much.
2. You can learn new things, but you can't really change how intelligent you are.
3. No matter how much intelligence you have, you can always change it quite a bit.
4. You can always substantially change how intelligent you are.

Dweck's Commentary: Statements 3 and 4 reflect the growth mindset. Which did you agree with more? You can be a mixture, but most people lean toward one or the other.

Set Two (Personal Qualities)

1. You are a certain kind of person, and there is not much that can be done to really change that.
2. No matter what kind of person you are, you can always change substantially.
3. You can do things differently, but the important parts of who you are can't really change.
4. You can always change basic things about the kind of person you are.

Dweck's commentary: Here, statements 1 and 3 are the fixed-mindset attributes and statements 2 and 4 reflect the growth mindset. Which did you agree with more? Did the personal qualities result differ from your intelligence qualities result? It can.[7]

I once coached a CEO who completed this exercise. Then the team followed suit. He shared his results and then they compared notes and had a greater understanding of their own "personal mindset trajectory," as well as that of the collective team. The findings follow. He had a challenge but was aware of his influence to impact his culture—beginning with himself—to become more proactive and an agile learner. He viewed this as an invitation for himself and his team to grow together, consciously striving, to model a growth mindset for the larger organization.

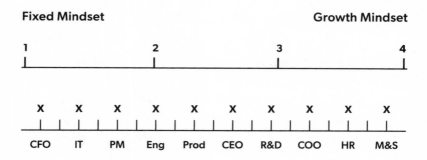

CFO = Chief Financial Officer
IT = Information Technology Director
PM = Project Management Director
Eng = Engineering Director

Prod = Production Manager

CEO = Chief Executive Officer

R&D = Research and Development Director

COO = Chief Operating Officer

HR = Human Resource Director

M&S = Marketing and Sales Director

Let's lighten up for a moment. In summary, when looking at this graph, you can see that the CFO has the least growth mindset on the team, almost in hugging distance from the IT director, whereas the M&S director has the strongest growth mindset, closely followed by HR. It is not surprising to see project management, production, and engineering prone to a fixed mindset. Imagine what marketing and sales go through every day! Or the frustration and stress that production, engineering, and project management must endure from M&S! The CEO is close to the middle. As the wind blows, what is the leader's predictable behavior, especially when he or she is up against it on actual versus forecast numbers and worried about cash flow?

Significantly, the COO is leaning more to a growth mindset. This is encouraging in light of the positional power vested in this role. HR is viewed as proactive and advocates personal development. This particular HR director has an understanding and appreciation of organizational development and is viewed as a change catalyst. R&D, which is really pre-engineering, is sacrosanct, referred to as the company's black box, and is frequently misunderstood as being an alien from a distant planet. Collectively, the company is a borderline 2.5—nearly in the middle.

The trajectory of the organization toward a growth mindset has yet to be determined. I feel it is moving in the right direction, and although I am biased, I am encouraged. These leaders are becoming more conscious of their influence to shape the mindset of their enterprise.

Now, where do *you* find yourself on the scale of the fixed as opposed to growth mindset? Where would your team members place their *X* on the continuum? Collectively, as a team, where would you place the *X*?

Now I will move the conversation from being a little playful to more contemplative. The pandemic that began spreading through America beginning in early 2020 resulted—more than ever—in the need for CEOs and their teams to further venture into the unknown by exploring and adopting the growth mindset. Leaders were forced to reflect as their states were locked down to reinforce social distancing in an attempt to stop the spread of COVID-19. Two questions they had to ponder: What are we learning about ourselves and each other? What are we now beginning to know through this period of not-knowing? They knew that their companies would not be alone, as their cities, states, country, and planet grappled with the unknown.

What mindset will your organization embrace as you and your team are faced with periods of uncertainty, complexity, and confusion? What stated values will you, as the CEO, espouse to your team, employees, customers, suppliers, and the community? What leadership behaviors do you expect from your team that will reinforce your organization's stated values and further differentiate your company's leadership posture in the external environment?

Let's return now to the Wisdom Life Chart.

Experience + Knowledge + Self Reflection = Wisdom

Like a musical score, it does not freeze a moment in time. It is not like a single-scene photograph. Instead, it flows on, movement after movement. To achieve the highest level of wisdom—referred to in the Old Testament Book of Proverbs as *Tushiya*, which gives one insight beyond the human and toward transcending and divine (spiritual) realities—one must be in motion. This forward, transparent movement imbues a transcendence, enabling you to step outside yourself and understand what is going on. Self-magnanimity takes hold, which gives one a sense of being okay, a sense of bliss, or a sunburst, even if you find yourself in upheaval or knee deep in muddy water. The *Experience* and the *Knowledge* and the *Reflection* renew and grow as ever-richer variations upon themes.

Further insight into the Wisdom Life Chart comes from the American philosopher Herbert Fingarette: "We are constitutive of our own experience, which crosses philosophy, theology and literary criticism."[8] Please note, the "Wisdom's Invitation" section near the end of this book encompasses Fingarette's entreaty. The selections, texts, books, and articles were foundational to the Wisdom Life Chart and to the role of the synthesist.

The Internal Change Agent/
The Aspiring Leader

The Vitruvian Man has been mentioned in this text more than twenty times now. Maybe you're not a man, or you don't fit the "executive stereotype." Is this really a book for you? The text has assumed an easy familiarity with business terminology, but maybe your own workspace has not been filled with C-suite furniture. And maybe, when surrounded by the assured jocularity of a country-club crowd, you've felt, well, out of place. Is this really a book for you?

Absolutely. Especially you. The insights, principles, exercises, challenges, and resources of *Alignment Strong* enable a potential or newly promoted leader to compete and to be involved with validity. You can advance while remaining balanced on genuine strengths, rather than inheriting your position. In this way, you will bring extra value to the organization.

If you are someone who has felt excluded within the organization's culture, a plus can be that you have paid special attention to how your organization's leadership has conducted their job. Keen observations of any shortcomings can mean you have a knowledgeable viewpoint for effective improvement. As stated early on in this book, to achieve Alignment Strong is to align one's personal vision, expectations, and unique contribution or personal value proposition to the organization's values, strategic vision, mission, and goals. Misalignment keeps both the individual and the organization from being potentialized. Without this individualized drive to alignment, the collective appetite for organizational change is stymied, as is the move to improve the organization's competitive edge.

Ideally, these things are happening: The enterprise is consciously creating the opportunity for you to align. Leadership is creating psychological safety. Vulnerability is a leadership norm emanating from the C-suite. Leadership is seriously and consistently engaging the members of the organization. Empathizing with the employees why they are at work gives them the sense of belonging, affirming their commitments, as espoused and practiced in the core values of the organization. The organization gives them the space to create meaning and find personal purpose.

Keeping in mind that this ideal picture may or may not exist, there is much discussion today on diversity and having diverse voices at the table. I'd like to suggest a more personalized approach to increase inclusion effectiveness organization-wide. The value of inclusion must be activated with personalization. This is really about personal philosophy, purpose, and meaning. Now, shifting back to the leader's perspective, he or she should not only be socially aware of this process, but should resonate proactiveness, transparency, and effectively utilize empathic listening skills to become a catalyst for this significant role.

Kimberley Barker stresses that a leader should want his or her employees to *feel* like they are part of the organizational "team"—knowing why they are at work, *feeling* like they make a difference—and that each voice can be heard and acknowledged and can really make an impact. Vernā Myers often says, "Diversity is being invited to the party; inclusion is being asked to dance."[1] Committed and active participation is very important. The courage to ask another person—possibly an unwilling or shy person—to dance is required. It is the only way to learn how to dance together. Yes, it does get personal. Vulnerability beckons, but what is a culture without a willingness to trust? Recalling my teenage years, the sheer act of asking one to dance spiked my anxiety, requiring an extra dose of courage. I still struggle with personal rejection to this day. I know how much courage it takes . . . but it can be done. As a leader or aspiring leader, you can do it.

I offer up anecdotal evidence related to the power of trust. For those interested in data, there's science to prove the point. A 2017 *Harvard Business Review* article, "The Neuroscience of Trust," highlights this: "A culture of trust is what makes a meaningful difference. Employees in high-trust organizations are more productive, have more energy at work, collaborate better with their colleagues, and stay with their employers longer than people working at low-trust companies."[2]

As part of testing their assumptions, the author and his colleagues traveled to many countries, including remote village communities. In the author's words: "We obtained permission to run experiments at numerous field sites where we measured oxytocin [brain chemical] and stress hormones and then assessed employees' productivity and ability to innovate. This research even took me to the rainforest of Papua New Guinea, where I measured oxytocin in indigenous people to see if the relationship between oxytocin and trust is universal. [It is.]" Of interest, the author and his colleagues simply asked this question: "How much do you enjoy your job on a daily basis?" The experiment, he wrote, shows that "having a greater sense of higher purpose stimulates oxytocin production, as does trust. Trust and purpose then mutually reinforce each other, providing a mechanism for extended oxytocin release, which produces happiness."

Sadly, most organizations' leadership fails to take an active personal role. Proactivity, ideally underscored by a culture of psychological safety and trust, suffers. And as an outsider on the inside, you may have become especially aware of where positive change needs to occur in leadership, team development, mission clarity, core values and/or strategy, strategic issue identification, and goal setting. In your role, all of these vantage points may be viewed as starting points to influence the organization.

You, too, can learn and astutely apply the vocabulary I've used and the ten components I have referred to in the earlier chapters. By utilizing these ideas, you will be far more astute. While building a coffee and chilies business in the remote rainforest of Papua New Guinea, I was faced with the stark reality of a region in which multiple languages were in use. As I entered one valley after another, dialects would completely change, forcing me to speak and then rely on three different sequential interpretations to effectively communicate. To access the C-suite and other power bastions requires much the same endeavor.

What I just described in the previous sentence is a tedious and incremental effort, akin to bricklaying (e.g., repeated attempts and interactions). It requires a willfulness to be vulnerable—to expose yourself. You will calculate the risk and reward. There will be wounds, misunderstandings, mistakes, and maybe a fiasco. Yet there will also be successes, quiet and intrinsic satisfaction, or possibly bliss. Will it be worth it, to sign up for the long haul?

Up to this point, the outsider I am referring to is obviously you. But we have much in common: I have been an outside/third-party change agent/ catalyst for about thirty years. Whether in a domestic or global application, I have observed very few organizational development professionals create personal social capital to access the C-suite. For me, it took a great effort, including courage and faith, to access the power base of thirty-five different villages in the Managalas Plateau, Oro Province, scattered over 125 square kilometers in Papua New Guinea. Painstakingly, I learned who was the village chief, clan chiefs, elders, sorcerers, which farmers owned the most land, and who had the largest gardens and most pigs.

I was confronted by the Tabuane village chief, Stafford. In my first open pavilion meeting, including fifty farmers, clan chiefs, and elders, he saluted me by using the name Tau Bada. It means big white man. He then asked why I was there. I did not respond immediately by reciting my work credentials, educational pedigree, religious convictions, or past accomplishments. No, with deliberate caution I said, "Because I want to be here."

I knew that I did not have to know. It was that simple. I had the hidden and unknown areas of the Johari Window panes on autopilot. I was unconsciously using them as my open area expanded with transparency and authenticity. Chief Stafford would have nabbed me on the spot as a charlatan if I had begun trying to convince him that I knew anything. That nanosecond of vulnerability was the tipping point. That was enough to connect with this wiry old chief, who really opened up the opportunity for his whole plateau to benefit immeasurably over the next seven years of our relationship. We became trusting friends. He did his part by including me in village sing-sings, village market day, funeral *haus krais* (house cries), weddings, and clan confrontations. I felt like I belonged. My experience was personal. This social capital can be gained by knowing the language of your organization, deftly applying it with self- and organizational awareness, resonating a transparency and self-confidence that you know or don't know what you are talking about, and being vulnerable enough to ask for help.

There is a transcending quality as well, another dimension, further deepening these important organizational relationships. Whether one chooses to label it spiritual, religious, existential, transformational, or all of these, a compassion, empathy, and love for others will spiral to the surface. We inevitably begin to comprehend, appreciate, and forgive ourselves and one another.

Also, a pragmatic orientation needs to be included for you, the internal change agent, to be effective. You must jump into the fishbowl, become a fish, and swim with the fish. Planting, cultivating, picking, and drying coffee beans with the farmers taught me a great deal, besides profusely perspiring. I dressed like them, ate with them, used the same pits (earthen toilets), acquired similar body odor, and washed in the rivers with them. You become more useful and indispensable to the organization as an agent of change.

Robert Putnam nuances the understanding of social capital and refers to "connections among individuals—social networks and the norms of reciprocity and trustworthiness that arise from them."[3] Without this connecting, which requires emotional and cognitive empathy and a holistic-systems perspective, the agent of change will not significantly accumulate social capital. Consequently, organizational development practitioners like myself are frequently characterized as too academic, impersonal, and rationalistic with their abundance of intellectual knowledge, learning models, training, and coaching programs.

I don't want to be misconstrued; this type of "intellectual capital" underpinned by a rational cause-and-effect orientation is valuable. But alone, without social capital, most of my colleagues' proposed change initiatives are often labeled as HR activities and training programs. As a result, you won't be admitted into where the power resides with only an intellectual pedigree, which, along with well-intentioned efforts, may gain recognition but will not be sufficient without adequate, well-earned social capital.

Without my earning the respect of the "village C-suites," we would not have been able to unify and align thirty-five villages to deliver two hundred tons per year of single-origin, shade-grown arabica certified organic and Rainforest Alliance coffee to the global market, especially without power, running water, or paved roads.

Now, getting back to you. If you accept this change catalyst role—possibly incognito!—how do you play it out successfully? For your first steps, I suggest you choose an area or seek an opportunity in which you can come across to your peers, subordinates, and management, not as excluded or representing a niche, but instead as someone feeling newly at home in the mainstream. Scan the organization for individuals who have excellent coaching/mentoring skills. Get close to them. Embody, without fanfare, your inclusion goal as your personal mission, ringing for you, with purpose and meaning. Let deep integrity resonate from you, as the bell tolls day after day. Before putting forth big suggestions to any of the constituents I just mentioned, ask questions such as, "In what specific ways can we best deal with this particular challenge, in the internal organization and/or the external environment?" Using "we" puts you on the side of unity in the pursuit of success. By doing so, you are bridging the dichotomized approach of "communitarianism" versus "individualism," as the writer Emanuele Ferragina explains.[4]

This book's intention is to present Alignment Strong as a competitive leadership framework. I bring myself into the equation as an ex-CEO, change agent, coach, and fellow learner. By expressing specific empathy for your challenges and sharing, at times, intimate experiences with you, I hope that this book resonates on an even deeper level than most, which will hopefully make a dent in your possibly overloaded mind.

Final Thoughts

Wisdom generally does not arrive in a flash, like inspiration. It is cumulative. As expressed in the Wisdom Life Chart, at any point in your life, wisdom is the sum of experience, knowledge, and self-reflection *so far*. You really have to live a while to acquire wisdom (as recognized in something as simple as the term "wisdom teeth," so called because they arrive around the time an adolescent takes on adult responsibilities).

Over the years, I've found self-reflection on the road, in motion. My motorcycled miles have included biking through unrelenting rainstorms, all-day 35-mile-an-hour crosswinds, fogged mountain passes, and, tragically, coming upon two fatal motorcycle accidents. I had to weather the sleet and storms, ride through the obstacles, and face my fears. Just as you must do as a leader.

My journeys—my vision quests, if you will—have included incredible treks under extraordinary, silhouetted cloud formations, past the scents of forests, sage and flowers and freshly mowed fields, and the sounds of loons, roosters, frogs, and crickets; rustling winds, sunrises, azure sky, and sunsets; friendly ranchers, irreverent cowboys, transcendent Native Americans, advice-giving bartenders and patrons; and surprise appearances by eagles, hawks, deer, coyotes, badgers, and ravens.

All of this individuality—stressful or beautiful; in nature or in humanity—provides the living frame in which I ruminate on my wisdom so far. And what I've learned is this: True leadership is looking within; finding the courage to ask the hard questions of yourself, to find your blind spots, to discover, not to fear change. Vulnerability is the essence of self. It is a strength that translates into your business and your life. Align yourself and align your business; find your plumb line; anchor yourself in vulnerability. Once you do that, plug in the ten components of this book. That's the simple organizational code. Visualize the components' strengths on the schematic and you will become the ideal leader of the ideal organization. Da Vinci's Vitruvian Man—gender-free—symbolizes the ideal in *all* of us.

WISDOM'S INVITATION

offer credit to the following books and articles—organized alphabetically by author within the Wisdom Life Chart structure—that inspired me, and an invitation to you to read (or reread) them in a way that adds up to your greater **Wisdom**.

EXPERIENCE

The Arbinger Institute, *Leadership and Self-Deception: Getting Out of the Box* (2000)

Joel Barker, *Paradigms: The Business of Discovering the Future* (1993)

James MacGregor Burns, *Leadership* (1978)

Joseph Campbell, *The Hero with a Thousand Faces* (1949)

Joseph Campbell, *The Hero's Journey: Joseph Campbell on His Life and Work (The Collected Works of Joseph Campbell)* (2014)

Harvey Cox, *The Future of Faith* (2009)

David L. Dotlich and Peter C. Cairo, *Why CEOs Fail* (2003)

Peter F. Drucker, *Management: Tasks, Responsibilities, Practices (1974)* and *Managing in Turbulent Times* (1980)

Gerard Egan, *Working the Shadow Side: A Guide to Positive Behind-the-Scenes Management* (1994)

Loren Eiseley, *The Immense Journey: An Imaginative Naturalist Explores the Mysteries of Man and Nature* (1957)

Catherine Fitzgerald and Linda K. Kirby, *Developing Leaders: Research and Applications in Psychological Type and Leadership Development* (1997)

Viktor Frankl, *Man's Search for Meaning* (1946)

Kelin E. Gersick, John Davis, Marion McCollom Hampton, and Ivan Lansberg, *Generation to Generation: Life Cycles of the Family Business* (1997)

James Gleick, *Chaos: Making a New Science* (1987)

Edward T. Hall, *Beyond Culture* (1976)

Michael Hammer, *The Agenda: What Every Business Must Do to Dominate the Decade* (2001)

James Hillman, *The Soul's Code: In Search of Character and Calling* (1997)

Eric Hoffer, *The True Believer: Thoughts on the Nature of Mass Movements* (1951)

Robert Kegan, *The Evolving Self: Problem and Process in Human Development* (1982)

Jack Kerouac, *On the Road* (1957)

King James Version, *Holy Bible* (1611)

Daniel J. Levinson, *The Seasons of a Man's Life* (1978)

Alexander Lowen, *Narcissism: Denial of the True Self* (1984)

Niccolo Machiavelli, *The Prince* (1532)

W. Somerset Maugham, *The Razor's Edge* (1944)

Thomas Moore, *The Education of the Heart* (1997) and *Dark Nights of the Soul: A Guide to Finding Your Way Through Life's Ordeals* (2004)

Gareth Morgan, *Images of Organization* (2007)

Peg C. Neuhauser, *Tribal Warfare in Organizations* (1988)

Flannery O'Connor, *The Complete Stories* (1971)

Kerry Patterson et al., *Influencer: The Power to Change Anything* (2007)

Eugene H. Peterson, *The Message* (2002)

Robert Pirsig, *Zen and the Art of Motorcycle Maintenance: An Inquiry into Values* (1974)

W. Brendan Reddy and Kaleel Jamison, *Team Building: Blueprints for Productivity and Satisfaction* (1988)

Monty Roberts, *The Man Who Listens to Horses* (1997)

Edgar H. Schein, *Helping: How to Offer, Give, and Receive Help* (2009)

Edgar Schein and Peter Schein, *Humble Leadership: The Power of Relationships, Openness, and Trust* (2018)

Peter Senge, *The Fifth Discipline Fieldbook: Strategies and Tools for Building a Learning Organization* (1994)

Huston Smith, *The Way Things Are* (2003)

Sun Tzu, *The Art of War* (1913)

Paul Tillich, *The Courage to Be* (1952)

Eckhart Tolle, *The Power of Now: A Guide to Spiritual Enlightenment* (1997)

Etienne Wenger, William Snyder, and Richard McDermott, *Cultivating Communities of Practice: A Guide to Managing Knowledge* (2002)

KNOWLEDGE

Peter Block, *The Empowered Manager: Positive Political Skills at Work* (1987) and *Flawless Consulting: A Guide to Getting Your Expertise Used* (1987)

David G. Bowers, *Systems of Organization: Management of the Human Resource* (1976)

Daniel Denison et al., *Leading Culture Change in Global Organizations* (2012)

Max De Pree, *Leadership Is an Art* (1989)

Catherine Fitzgerald and Jennifer Garvey Berger, *Executive Coaching: Practices & Perspectives* (2002)

Wendell L. French and Cecil Bell, *Organization Development: Behavioral Science Interventions for Organization Improvement* (1984)

Daniel Goleman, *Emotional Intelligence* (1995); and Daniel Goleman, Richard Boyatzis, and Annie McKee, *Primal Leadership: Realizing the Power of Emotional Intelligence* (2002)

Calvin S. Hall et al., *Introduction to Theories of Personality* (1985)

Jim Haudan and Rich Berens, *What Are Your Blind Spots? Conquering the 5 Misconceptions that Hold Leaders Back* (2018)

Edgar F. Huse, *Organization Development and Change* (1980)

Alan Jacobs, *How to Think: A Survival Guide for a World at Odds* (2017)

Rosabeth Moss Kanter, *The Change Masters: Innovation & Entrepreneurship in the American Corporation* (1983)

James Kouzes and Barry Posner, *Credibility: How Leaders Gain and Lose It, Why People Demand It* (1993)

Frederic Laloux, *Reinventing Organizations* (2014)

Patrick Lencioni, *The Five Dysfunctions of a Team* (1998) and *Getting Naked: A Business Fable About Shedding the Three Fears that Sabotage Client Loyalty* (2010)

Joan Magretta, *Understanding Michael Porter: The Essential Guide to Competition and Strategy* (2011)

Cormac McCarthy, *Blood Meridian* (1985)

Stephen Covey, *The Speed of Trust* (2006)

Henry Mintzberg, *The Rise and Fall of Strategic Planning* (1994); *The Structuring of Organizations* (1989); Mintzberg et al., *Strategy Safari: A Guided Tour Through the Wilds of Strategic Management* (1998)

Thomas Peters and Robert H. Waterman Jr., *In Search of Excellence* (1982)

Michael E. Porter, *Competitive Advantage: Creating and Sustaining Superior Performance* (1985) and *Competitive Strategy: Techniques for Analyzing Industries and Competitors* (1980)

Anne Rød and Marita Fridjhon, *Creating Intelligent Teams* (2016)

Marshall Sashkin, *Organizational Behavior: Concepts and Experiences* (1984)

Edgar H. Schein, *Organizational Culture and Leadership* (1985) and *Process Consultation: Its Role in Organization Development* (1999)

Jay M. Shafritz, J. Steven Ott, and Yong Suk Jang, *Classics of Organization Theory* (1978)

James Thompson, *Organizations in Action: Social Science Bases of Administrative Theory* (1967)

Noel Tichy, *The Leadership Engine: How Winning Companies Build Leaders at Every Level* (1997)

John Ward, *Perpetuating the Family Business: 50 Lessons Learned from Long-Lasting, Successful Families in Business* (2004)

Marvin R. Weisbord, *Organizational Diagnosis: A Workbook of Theory and Practice* (1978) and *Productive Workplaces: Dignity, Meaning, and Community in the 21st Century* (2012)

SELF/SOCIAL REFLECTION

Richard Attenborough, *The Words of Gandhi* (1982)

Don Beck and Christopher Cowan, *Spiral Dynamics: Mastering Values, Leadership, and Change* (1996)

David G. Benner, *The Gift of Being Yourself* (2015)

Marcus J. Borg, *Convictions: How I Learned What Matters Most* (2014)

John Bradshaw, *The Family* (1985)

William Bridges with Susan Bridges, *Managing Transitions: Making the Most of Change* (1991)

David Brooks, *The Road to Character* (2015)

Jim Collins, *Good to Great: Why Some Companies Make the Leap . . . and Others Don't* (2001)

Jared Diamond, *Collapse: How Societies Choose to Fail or Succeed* (2005)

Carol S. Dweck, *Mindset: The New Psychology of Success* (2006)

Robert Fritz, *The Path of Least Resistance for Managers* (1999)

Robert Frost, *Sweet and Bitter Bark: Selected Poems* (1992)

Gary Hamel, *The Future of Management* (2007)

Allen F. Harrison and Robert Bramson, *The Art of Thinking* (2002)

Jim Harrison, *The Theory & Practice of Rivers and New Poems* (1989)

John Hart, *Heroes and Progresses: Studies in American Literature* (1985)

Chungliang Al Huang and Jerry Lynch, *Mentoring: The Tao of Giving and Receiving Wisdom* (1995)

Søren Kierkegaard, *Purity of Heart Is to Will One Thing* (1847)

Laozi, *Tao Te Ching* (1954)

Gordon Marino, *The Existentialist's Survival Guide: How to Live Authentically in an Inauthentic Age* (2018)

William Martin, *The Tao of Forgiveness: The Healing Power of Forgiving Others and Yourself* (2010)

Robert Moore, *Facing the Dragon: Confronting Personal and Spiritual Grandiosity* (2003)

John O'Donohue, *Anam Cara: A Book of Celtic Wisdom* (1997)

Daniel H. Pink, *A Whole New Mind: Why Right-Brainers Will Rule the Future* (2005)

Steven Pinker, *The Better Angels of Our Nature: Why Violence Has Declined* (2011)

Bill Plotkin, *Nature and the Human Soul: Cultivating Wholeness and Community in a Fragmented World* (2007)

Jeremy Rifkin, *The Empathic Civilization: The Race to Global Consciousness in a World in Crisis* (2010)

Richard Rohr, *Falling Upward* (2011)

Rumi (translated by Coleman Barks), *The Essential Rumi* (expanded edition, 2004)

Donald Schon, *The Reflective Practitioner: How Professionals Think in Action* (1983)

Will Schutz, *Profound Simplicity* (1979)

Elton Trueblood, *The Humor of Christ* (1964)

The list may feel overwhelming, but it is here in fullness to acknowledge what has come before us, as well as to offer possibilities for further inspiration. In that spirit of a formal acknowledgement, let's also credit/propose some shorter pieces of reading. The following are from the *Harvard Business Review.*

Michael Beer, Magnus Finnstrom, and Derek Schrader, "Building a Workforce for the Future," October 2016.

Marcus Buckingham and Ashley Goodall, "Reinventing Performance Management," April 2015.

Claudio Fernández-Aráoz, Andrew Roscoe, and Kentaro Aramaki, "Turning Potential into Success: The Missing Link in Leadership Development," November/December 2017.

Daniel Goleman, "Leadership That Gets Results," March 2000; "The Focused Leader," December 2013.

Boris Groysberg, Jeremiah Lee, Jesse Price, and J. Yo-Jud Cheng, "The Leader's Guide to Corporate Culture," January/February 2018.

Rosabeth Moss Kanter, "What Would Peter Say?," November 2009.

Roger L. Martin, "The Big Lie of Strategic Planning," January-February 2014.

In examining these books and articles, you've probably been reflecting on what you have previously read, what you already know, and your own particular inclinations for further learning. In this process, I suggest being particularly open to examining the books and articles in these listings that you find *least* attractive. Not least relevant, but least attractive. Even a relatively brief perusal of them will, by the challenge, sharpen your inner articulations, enlarge your ability to be vulnerable, and add to your wisdom. Practically speaking, such a process will enable you to be a more effective leader. You can then lean into your fears, your resistance, and become Alignment Strong.

Acknowledgments

I would like to thank my soul partner, Fiona, who has helped me through the surges and storms, and stilled the waters of my Writers Tears; our daughters, Jasmine, Kaia, and Mahealani, who are embarking on their own adventures and provide me with expanded and different perspectives; my brothers, Patrick, Jim, and Jack; my sister, Diane, for being there throughout my life; and my many friends, mentors, and teachers, without whom I would not be who I am today.

Appendix

This section has eight self-administering exercises for leaders and their teams. My clients have found such tools highly valuable.

1. The **Alignment Strong Assessment** allows you to reflect on what you have read and complete your evaluation of the Da Vinci Organizational Code's ten components. This is a concrete way to evaluate how your organization and the Alignment Strong process match up—or could.

2. The **Mission Statement Development Procedure and Evaluation** demonstrates why and how, even if top management itself is highly able and experienced, a soundly constructed mission statement is hugely valuable to an organization. The exercise will help you build, reshape, or critique your own.

3. Use the **Leadership Development Questionnaire** to assess the critical skills required for you to effectively execute your leadership and management roles. A strong leader keeps all ten components aligned in order to adapt to the external environment.

4. **Essential Team Factors and Team Assessment**, attributed to Bruce Gibb, PhD, is a sound, easily understood, yet

comprehensive team development narrative and evaluation. It should be a handy instrument in your developmental toolbox.

5. **Role Definition Development** will assist in eliminating role conflict between individuals as well as role ambiguity for each person, resulting in increased effectiveness and efficiency. A clear role definition is a fundamental requirement to optimize individual performance, increase job satisfaction, add value as a team member, and maximize one's role/function in the value chain. It is the underpinning of a performance management system. This role definition process will help evolve your role and others from an "as is" status to a "should be" status.

6. The **Team Development Exercise Module** is an exercise to increase team trust and reduce the fear of conflict by sharing with one another the team members' strengths, weaknesses, and blind spots. It is imperative for the CEO to develop a high-performance team. One may utilize Patrick Lencioni's Five Dysfunctions team model as a developmental framework by identifying what level of dysfunction the team is currently experiencing. This will create a group consensus and resolve. Team members will then give and receive critical feedback based on Daniel Goleman's *Emotional Intelligence* capabilities.

7. An example of a completed action plan of **Strategic Issue Definition, Goal Statement, and Objectives/Action Steps** will give you a better grasp of effective goal setting.

8. The **Goal/Action Plan Team Ratification Session** template reinforces the outcome for effective goal setting, which is accuracy. Additional benefits include the crossing over of potential organizational silos and affirming team member interdependency.

1. ALIGNMENT STRONG ASSESSMENT

Assess each of the ten components by circling one of the numbers (1–4), 4 being the highest for effectiveness, and 1 the lowest for effectiveness, relying on the descriptors under each number, as well as the response to the critical question. Then, with each component, explain why you gave it the ranking you did, followed by suggestions/recommendations for improvement, if warranted.

Core Values

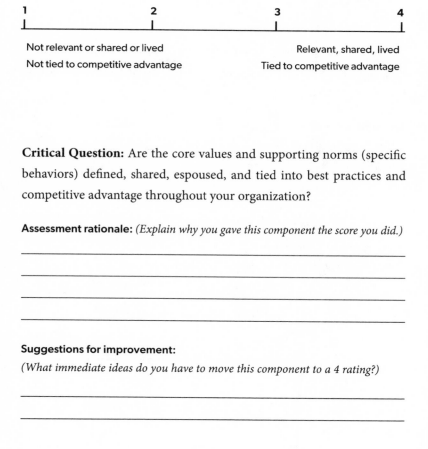

| 1 | 2 | 3 | 4 |

Not relevant or shared or lived
Not tied to competitive advantage

Relevant, shared, lived
Tied to competitive advantage

Critical Question: Are the core values and supporting norms (specific behaviors) defined, shared, espoused, and tied into best practices and competitive advantage throughout your organization?

Assessment rationale: *(Explain why you gave this component the score you did.)*

_____

_____

_____

_____

Suggestions for improvement:
(What immediate ideas do you have to move this component to a 4 rating?)

_____

_____

_____

_____

_____

_____

Strategic Vision

1	2	3	4

Not clear, revelant, or inspiring   Clear, relevant, and inspiring

Not aligned to core values   Aligned to core values

Critical Question: Does the company demonstrate its commitment to long-term growth through the formulation and articulation of a five-year strategic vision?

Assessment rationale: *(Explain why you gave this component the score you did.)*

_____

_____

_____

_____

Suggestions for improvement:

(What immediate ideas do you have to move this component to a 4 rating?)

_____

_____

_____

_____

Mission/Competitive Advantage

1	2	3	4

Not current, not relevant to existing
products/services
Competitive advantage
not understood

Current, relevant to
products/services
Competitive advantage
understood

Critical Question: Is the mission and competitive advantage of the organization clearly stated and understood organization-wide?

Assessment rationale: *(Explain why you gave this component the score you did.)*

_____

_____

_____

Suggestions for improvement:
(What immediate ideas do you have to move this component to a 4 rating?)

_____

_____

_____

Leadership/Team

1	2	3	4

Leadership (CEO) rarely seen or felt
Leadership and/or team credibility is low
Leadership is not adaptive/unresponsive
Formal team-building model/
process absent
Low performing team

Leadership (CEO) highly visible and felt
Leadership and/or team credibility is high
Leadership adaptive/responsive
Formal team-building model/
process utilized
High performing team

Critical Questions: Do you feel that leadership (CEO) and its commitment are felt and visible throughout the organization? Has top management modeled an effective team reflective of the CEO's leadership throughout the organization?

Assessment rationale: *(Explain why you gave this component the score you did.)*

_____

_____

_____

_____

Suggestions for improvement:
(What immediate ideas do you have to move this component to a 4 rating?)

_____

_____

_____

_____

Strategy

| 1 | 2 | 3 | 4 |

Narrative not formulated	Narrative concisely formulated
Consensus absent in C-suite	Consensus in C-suite
Not shared with management	Shared with management
Not aligned to values and strategic vision	Aligned to values and strategic vision

Critical Question: Does a strategy narrative exist and is it shared with management, rationalizing the enterprise's current competitive posture as well as prioritizing internal value chain preparedness in order to deliver/execute the stated mission (i.e., products and services) more effectively and efficiently than your rival's?

Assessment rationale: *(Explain why you gave this component the score you did.)*

_____

_____

_____

_____

Suggestions for improvement:
(What immediate ideas do you have to move this component to a 4 rating?)

_____

_____

_____

_____

Goals/Objectives

1	2	3	4

Not developed	Clearly developed
Uniform process absent	Uniform process in place
Not tied to roles and rewards	Tied to roles and rewards
Not aligned to values, vision,	Aligned to values, vision,
mission, and strategy	mission, and strategy

Critical Question: Does the current goal-setting process reinforce clarity/specificity, and high attainability and high participation, emboldening results throughout the organization?

Assessment rationale: *(Explain why you gave this component the score you did.)*

_____

_____

_____

_____

Suggestions for improvement:

(What immediate ideas do you have to move this component to a 4 rating?)

_____

_____

_____

_____

Organization Structure

1	2	3	4

Not rationalized for optimization   Rationalized for optimization

Role definitions unclear   Clear role definitions

Reporting relationships conflicted   Reporting relationships coherent

Not aligned to values/strategy   Aligned to values/strategy

Critical Questions: Does the organization's structure seem to be designed for the most effective and efficient use of its people and other resources? Are roles and reporting relationships clearly defined, understood, and shared?

Assessment rationale: *(Explain why you gave this component the score you did.)*

_____

_____

_____

_____

Suggestions for improvement:

(What immediate ideas do you have to move this component to a 4 rating?)

_____

_____

_____

_____

Departmental Mission Statements

1	2	3	4

Absent	Developed and clearly articulated
Disconnected to company mission	Highly connected to company mission
Frequent quality failures/missed deadlines	Exceeds quality expectations
Roles not supportive/low accountability	Roles engaged to execute mission
Low team results	High team results

Critical Questions: Are the organization-wide mission statements for departments and functions—clearly defined with specific outputs and deliverables, both internally and externally—supporting the stated corporate mission? Have the mission statements been vetted between departments/functions for comprehension to determine existing disconnects/bottlenecks, which would impair the delivery of products and services to one another, impacting the ultimate customer/end user?

Assessment rationale: *(Explain why you gave this component the score you did.)*

_____

_____

_____

_____

Suggestions for improvement:

(What immediate ideas do you have to move this component to a 4 rating?)

_____

_____

_____

_____

Individual Objectives/Management Performance System

1	2	3	4

Goals and objectives not individualized	Individual goals and objectives set
Lack of coaching from manager	Consistent coaching from manager
Avoidance of conflict/poor accountability	Conflict resolution/strong accountability
Absence of performance management	Uniform performance management
Not aligned to values, missions, and goals	Aligned to values, missions, and goals

Critical Question: Has the organization developed a performance management system establishing a strong link between personal development and individual performance, and rewards?

Assessment rationale: *(Explain why you gave this component the score you did.)*

_____

_____

_____

_____

Suggestions for improvement:

(What immediate ideas do you have to move this component to a 4 rating?)

_____

_____

_____

_____

Integrated Culture

1	2	3	4

Core values not integrated, developed, and/or not clearly stated	Core values clearly stated, espoused, and lived
Strategic vision and mission(s) not formally developed and/or clear	Strategic vision and mission(s) are developed and articulated
Leadership styles not responsive/ adaptive to culture	Responsive/adaptive leadership
Leadership (CEO) - team low credibility	Leadership (CEO) - team high credibility
Organization structure unresponsive to marketplace	Responsive organization structure
Goal setting - management performance practices absent and/or inconsistent	Goal setting - management performance practices consistent
Employees are not engaged/ not purposed	Employees are engaged/purposed
Fixed mindset/low learning agility	Growth mindset/high learning agility
Culture weakly aligned/out of sync with external environment	Culture strongly aligned/in sync with external environment

Critical questions: Assessing the present culture and current external environment, are the other nine Alignment Strong components understood organization-wide and integrated? Is the CEO's leadership style in sync with the organization's culture and demands of the external environment?

Assessment rationale: *(Explain why you gave this component the score you did.)*

_____

_____

_____

Suggestions for improvement:
(What immediate ideas do you have to move this component to a 4 rating?)

_____

_____

_____

ALIGNMENT ASSESSMENT SCORING

For every 4-point ranking per component, give yourself 10 points

For every 3-point ranking per component, give yourself 7.5 points

For every 2-point ranking per component, give yourself 5 points

For every 1-point ranking per component, give yourself 2.5 points

Now add them up and assess Alignment Strong for your organization.

100 points: you are an impeccably aligned organization worthy of a *Harvard Business Review* (HBR) case study

75 to 99 points: you are strongly aligned but should tweak your organization

50 to 74 points: you are only moderately aligned and in need of improvement

49 points or less: your organization may be heading into or is already in dire straits

2. MISSION STATEMENT DEVELOPMENT PROCEDURE AND EVALUATION

Corporate Mission/Competitive Advantage:
The Intangible Contributor to Performance

In the following scenario, the CEO and core team of a corporation had been engaged in a long-term effort to make their company more productive and profitable in an increasingly competitive market. After more than a year of right-sizing, stepped-up marketing and planning, and special training for top management in better management practices, improvements in market share, profits, and productivity were not measuring up to expectations.

The CEO wanted to know why. Significant surveying and interviewing at all levels of management within the company revealed that

- **85 percent** of all surveyed managers did not believe that the company's structure supported decision making.
- **57 percent** of management reported that communications and feedback were hindered by official channels—the bureaucracy.
- **Two-thirds** of all respondents did not believe organizational policies and procedures were applied consistently.
- **77 percent** of the managers did not see a link between strategic-level planning and decision making.
- **55 percent** of management did not believe that top management had established a leadership style that contributed to high employee morale and performance.

Not all the information gathered was negative. The CEO and his core team were deemed good professionals with verified accomplishments and performance records. Nevertheless, the most telling findings of the survey were

- **94 percent** of the surveyed management/supervisory level said there was not a clear corporate mission, a competitive advantage statement, nor a business plan for the company.
- Further, those managers felt that the absences of a mission, competitive advantage statement, and business plan were major impediments to the company's ability to compete and improve staff productivity. The company was like a ship without a rudder. And even the most competent executive team will have trouble steering a proper course for its company unless it is able to develop a mission that

  - Addresses the employees' needs to understand what the company is about and where it is going
  - Forges employee commitment to the company by establishing a set of values with which everyone can identify
  - Supports organization-wide productivity

The preceding description was articulated not more than a decade ago and might be viewed now as statistically unsound and anecdotal at best. Yet, not surprisingly, this accounting has not changed that much even today. Year after year, company after company, nearly the same findings come out in the initial sensing-assessment phase I undertake with new clients.

Arriving at the Best Mission Statement

Your mission statement should be a very carefully worded paragraph that amplifies your competitive advantage. It places emphasis on those concepts and actions the company intends to exploit as it implements its strategic plan. Employees who read the mission statement should be able to quickly comprehend where the company is placing its priorities and where it is focusing organizational effort to achieve the desired results.

A good mission statement usually does not exceed seventy-five words. Typically, it is a series of independent clauses, separated by semicolons. Points of emphasis appearing in the statement should be sequenced from the most important to the least important. The entire statement should be written in active voice. The company should be able to point to a specific action or program that is being or will be undertaken as a result of a mission statement commitment.

Generally, mission statements will indicate commitments to one or more of the following:

1. Type of growth desired (e.g., rapid, moderate, conservative)
2. Nature of the markets served (e.g., industrial, private label, consumer)
3. Product functional characteristics and/or definition
4. Profitability orientation
5. Market and/or product diversifications (breadth or narrowness)
6. The extent of emphasis on present company capabilities
7. Commitment to serve with some definition of the meaning of service
8. Geographical scope of the business (e.g., local, regional, national, multinational)
9. Customer orientation
10. Technical superiority

Departmental/Functional Mission Statements

These statements are developed by manufacturing, finance, IT, and marketing/sales departments to reflect each function's commitment to, and operationalization of, the corporate mission statement. The formulation of the departmental mission statements may be identical to the corporate mission statement OR they may be stated as a series of critical outputs/deliverables that each function identifies as key to the successful implementation of the corporate mission.

Corporate and Departmental Mission Statement Development

1. Identify, list, and prioritize external and internal customers/ stakeholders.

2. Identify, list, define, and prioritize products and services, which you will deliver and/or not deliver to identified customers.

3. Identify and define standards/benchmarks (e.g., timelines, cost quality, etc.), to which you will hold yourself accountable.

4. Rationalize and define a value proposition—the competitive advantage—in which products and services are consistently delivered at a lower cost and/or demand a higher price, which your competitors will struggle to match. Now defined, the pricing strategy has been more thoroughly rationalized. This cache of information is a critical component of the strategy and strategic plan.

5. Synthesis: Develop/pull together your thoughts into a statement of

   A. Who you are, who you serve, what you will do, and, therefore, not do; and what standards distinguish you.

B. Script out your competitive advantage statement and include it in your mission statement.

MISSION CLARITY EVALUATION

External and Internal Customers

1	2	3	4

| Unclear | | | Very clear |
| Confusing | | | Understood |

Products and Services

1	2	3	4

Ambiguous			Unambiguous
Not identified			Identified
Not understood			Clearly understood

Standards and Benchmarks

1	2	3	4

| Ambivalent | | | Unambivalent |
| Weak | | | Strong |

Competitive Advantage (Differentiation)

1	2	3	4

Not convincing   Convincing
Questionable value   Unquestionable value
Value/pricing unjustified   Value/pricing justified

Statement Coherency/Comprehensiveness

1	2	3	4

General   Specific
Generic   Customized
Fuzzy   Clear

3. LEADERSHIP DEVELOPMENT QUESTIONNAIRE

I use this questionnaire when beginning a developmental process that will lead to a mutual commitment for an executive coaching relationship. The relevancy of the subject material and cognitive tools is critical in light of the Alignment Strong model. Listed here is a set of thirty-six skills and management tools executives possess that they can utilize at one time or another.

The way to benefit from this form is to go through it four times.

First, look at the thirty-six skills/tools and determine how often you use each one. In the "frequency usage" column, write a 1, 2, or 3 for each.

1 = I rely on this skill often, feeling very confident to use it.

2 = I rely on this skill infrequently, feeling somewhat confident to use it.

3 = I rarely rely on this skill, not feeling confident to use it.

Next, go through the form using the second column, rating your ability to perform each skill.

0 = I don't know how to do this.

1 = I can do this but just barely. I need a lot of help.

2 = I feel confident that I do this well.

3 = I do this very well and could help others improve in their ability.

4 = I can do this exceptionally well, and I can teach others to do it.

Then use the "priority selection" column to rate each skill regarding its importance for you.

1 = Essential, top priority

2 = Useful and needed

3 = Helpful, but low priority

Finally, using the decisions you made in filling out the "priority selection" column, go on to the Top 10 Skills for You—and Why portion of the form and list the 10 skills most important for you, from highest to next-highest and so on, and explain your reasoning.

Executive Skills/Knowledge Assessment

	Frequency Usage	Rate Your Skill Level	Priority Selection
1. Formulate and articulate a compelling strategic vision of what the organization will be like in the future	_____	_____	_____
2. Have widespread agreement about the vision and supporting goals	_____	_____	_____
3. Ascertain/define an adaptive and clear organization structure (i.e., roles and reporting relationships)	_____	_____	_____
4. Formulate a clear, comprehensive mission and competitive advantage	_____	_____	_____
5. Communicate effectively among functions, departments, and divisions in order to minimize conflict and increase collaboration	_____	_____	_____
6. Strategically think, as opposed to problem solving and planning, by utilizing dialogue techniques	_____	_____	_____

	Frequency Usage	Rate Your Skill Level	Priority Selection
7. Employ integrative/inclusive strategic planning in order to reinforce long-term purpose and achieve short-term objectives	_____	_____	_____
8. Have a personal development focus on emotional intelligence and competence (i.e., self-confidence, empathy, openness, positive mindset, and high self-awareness)	_____	_____	_____
9. Develop effective management of stakeholder relationships	_____	_____	_____
10. Understand and utilize personal power to positively impact others to achieve organization/ institutional goals and a high-morale climate	_____	_____	_____
11. Formal goal setting/action planning	_____	_____	_____
12. Apply a value chain framework and methodology to enhance productivity, reduce costs, and increase profits with all departments/functions	_____	_____	_____
13. Tie individual goals to the economic drivers of the organization	_____	_____	_____
14. Exhibit effective coaching, counseling, and mentoring skills	_____	_____	_____

	Frequency Usage	Rate Your Skill Level	Priority Selection
15. Utilize the best information available to make good decisions	_____	_____	_____
16. Assert greater emotional control over difficult situations or conflicts	_____	_____	_____
17. Organize selection, progression, and succession planning	_____	_____	_____
18. Define/clarify personal and organizational core values to reinforce a high-performance culture	_____	_____	_____
19. Establish personal and organizational change management and transition techniques	_____	_____	_____
20. Demand management capability to hold individuals accountable to goals, objectives, and procedures	_____	_____	_____
21. Give negative and positive feedback to subordinates, peers, and managers	_____	_____	_____
22. Improve and maintain employee performance and/or work habits	_____	_____	_____
23. Motivate, reward, and sanction employees	_____	_____	_____

	Frequency Usage	Rate Your Skill Level	Priority Selection
24. Develop relevant and accurate role definitions and performance standards for direct reports	_____	_____	_____
25. Delegate responsibility to reinforce decision making throughout the organization	_____	_____	_____
26. Demonstrate effective management through an accountability and coaching process that will track individual performance	_____	_____	_____
27. Conduct an effective meeting	_____	_____	_____
28. Build high-performance and diverse teams to get things accomplished versus using a traditional hierarchy	_____	_____	_____
29. Increase conflict-resolution skills	_____	_____	_____
30. Develop your leadership and management profiles for the organization in order to exemplify change	_____	_____	_____
31. Build an empowered organization where risk-taking is encouraged and rewarded	_____	_____	_____

	Frequency Usage	Rate Your Skill Level	Priority Selection
32. Develop a culture where all members will have a deeper understanding of customer needs and wants	_____	_____	_____
33. Create a strong, adaptive, and high-performing culture to increase commitment	_____	_____	_____
34. Develop the capabilities and skills of people so they are viewed as an important source of competitive advantage	_____	_____	_____
35. Utilize financial/accounting information for annual planning, budgeting, and forecasting	_____	_____	_____
36. Have a greater understanding of the financial function, including credit and debt financing, recapitalization, and mergers and acquisition knowledge	_____	_____	_____

Top Ten Skills for You—and Why

1.   Number and name of skill:

_____

Supporting rationale:

_____

_____

_____

_____

2.   Number and name of skill:

_____

Supporting rationale:

_____

_____

_____

_____

3.   Number and name of skill:

_____

Supporting rationale:

_____

_____

_____

_____

4. Number and name of skill:

_____

Supporting rationale:

_____

_____

_____

_____

5. Number and name of skill:

_____

Supporting rationale:

_____

_____

_____

_____

6. Number and name of skill:

_____

Supporting rationale:

_____

_____

_____

_____

7. Number and name of skill:

_____

Supporting rationale:

_____

_____

_____

_____

8. Number and name of skill:

_____

Supporting rationale:

_____

_____

_____

_____

9. Number and name of skill:

_____

Supporting rationale:

_____

_____

_____

_____

10. Number and name of skill:

_____

Supporting rationale:

_____

_____

_____

_____

From this exercise you do not arrive at a numerical total telling where you are. Instead, through the four quantifying steps that you took and the rationales you wrote, you will gain substantial clarity about yourself and your organization in terms of leadership.

4. ESSENTIAL TEAM FACTORS AND TEAM ASSESSMENT

A team can often accomplish more than the same number of individuals working alone. The morale of team members who work together effectively is often higher than that of individuals working alone. Supervisors who know when it is appropriate to use a team—who know how to build or develop a team from a group of individuals—are very valuable assets to an organization.

Team development refers to any planned activity or series of events that develop or improve the team's ability to function. There is no one best way to develop a team. There is, however, a set of factors all teams spend time and energy developing. These factors always exist when two or more people have to work together to get a job done. Confusion or conflict in any of the areas can drain time and energy that could be devoted to the task. Effective teams deal with these issues consciously and proactively as opposed to leaving everything up to habit or in reaction to a crisis. The factors relating to team functioning are capsulized in the following questions.

1. **Mission:** What is the team trying to do? Who do you serve, and what are you going to deliver to your customers?

2. **Roles:** Who is required to do what in order to accomplish those tasks?

3. **Procedures:** How can people work together most effectively in performing their roles?

4. **Resources:** What skills, information, materials, and equipment are needed?

5. **Performance:** How well is the team performing its task (look at output and morale)?

6. **Relationships:** How do team members get along with each other?

7. **Organization:** Does the organization support teamwork?

In determining answers to these questions, it is important to remember that there is no one best answer or set of answers that applies to all teams. There are, however, some qualities associated with the preceding factors listed that can be worked on in order to improve team functioning.

1. **MISSION** (Do we all know who we serve with what output; why it is we are here to work together?)
   A. Clear
   B. Shared
   C. Operational goals and output goals
   D. Owned (by individuals and/or team)

2. **ROLES** (Are we clear about *who* we expect to be doing what?)
   A. Clear
   B. Unconflicted
   C. Overloaded with tasks and responsibilities
   D. Disagreement with others' expectations
   E. Disagreement with own expectations

3. **PROCEDURES** (Do we all know *how* we are going to work together?)
   A. Share information
   B. Plan and coordinate our work
   C. Make decisions; obtain input from others
   D. Valid, complete information
   E. Acceptance of decision by team members
   F. Timely decisions
   G. Hold meetings
   H. Communicate with each other
   I. Use conflict constructively
   J. Solve problems
   K. Organize/innovate our work more effectively and efficiently

4. **RESOURCES** (Do we have everything we need to produce excellent outputs?)

   A. Team members' abilities, skills, and knowledge (energy, emotions, values, and personality)

   B. Information for setting goals, monitoring, and evaluating performance

   C. Physical facilities, equipment, tools, and space (adequate, safe, maintained)

   D. Right materials at right place at right time

5. **PERFORMANCE** (How well do we perform as a team?)

   A. Quality, quantity, timeliness, and cost of the group's output

   B. Pride and satisfaction of the individual members with group's performance, other team members, their compensation, and their individual contribution to the team effort

6. **RELATIONSHIPS** (How well do team members get along with each other?)

   A. Friendly and attentive

   B. Personality conflicts

   C. Harmony

   D. Confidence

   E. Group morale

7. **ORGANIZATION** (Are we working in a system that makes it possible for real teamwork to exist?)

   A. Organization rewards team performance

   B. Organizational policies, procedures, and structure support teams

   C. Cross-team conflict resolved

Remember that a team does not exist in a vacuum. It is part of a larger system that may be stable or changing. Thus it is important to understand the team's organizational environment in order to realistically define Mission, Roles, Procedures, Resources, Performance, Relationships, and Organization.

Team Assessment

Please answer the following questions about how you, your co-workers, and your supervisor work together. The phrase "the team" refers to the persons sitting around the table with you today.

(Each question starts with "To what extent..." therefore, it is repeated at the top of the section but not for each question.)

Select the appropriate number to answer; this is how it is now (N), and this is how I would like it to be (L).

EXAMPLE
Questions:

1. MISSION To what extent . . .		**1** To a very little extent	**2** To a little extent	**3** To some extent	**4** To a good extent	**5** To a great extent
A. Does the team have a clear team mission or purpose?	N	☐ 1	☐ 2	☐ 3	☐ 4	☐ 5
	L	☐ 1	☐ 2	☐ 3	☐ 4	☐ 5
B. Does this team have clear team goals and objectives?	N	☐ 1	☐ 2	☐ 3	☐ 4	☐ 5
	L	☐ 1	☐ 2	☐ 3	☐ 4	☐ 5
C. Does everyone seem to agree on these team goals and objectives?	N	☐ 1	☐ 2	☐ 3	☐ 4	☐ 5
	L	☐ 1	☐ 2	☐ 3	☐ 4	☐ 5
D. Are you involved in setting goals and objectives for your team?	N	☐ 1	☐ 2	☐ 3	☐ 4	☐ 5
	L	☐ 1	☐ 2	☐ 3	☐ 4	☐ 5
E. Do members of this team work toward team goals and objectives?	N	☐ 1	☐ 2	☐ 3	☐ 4	☐ 5
	L	☐ 1	☐ 2	☐ 3	☐ 4	☐ 5
F. Do persons in this team encourage each other to give their best efforts?	N	☐ 1	☐ 2	☐ 3	☐ 4	☐ 5
	L	☐ 1	☐ 2	☐ 3	☐ 4	☐ 5
G. Does the team have shared performance standards—quality, quantity, cost—and schedule for team output?	N	☐ 1	☐ 2	☐ 3	☐ 4	☐ 5
	L	☐ 1	☐ 2	☐ 3	☐ 4	☐ 5

Questions:

2. ROLES
To what extent . . .

		1 To a very little extent	2 To a little extent	3 To some extent	4 To a good extent	5 To a great extent
A. Is your own job clearly defined?	N	☐ 1	☐ 2	☐ 3	☐ 4	☐ 5
	L	☐ 1	☐ 2	☐ 3	☐ 4	☐ 5
B. Do you have the authority you need to carry out your responsibilities?	N	☐ 1	☐ 2	☐ 3	☐ 4	☐ 5
	L	☐ 1	☐ 2	☐ 3	☐ 4	☐ 5
C. Do members of this team agree about who should do what job?	N	☐ 1	☐ 2	☐ 3	☐ 4	☐ 5
	L	☐ 1	☐ 2	☐ 3	☐ 4	☐ 5
D. Do members of this team agree what you should be doing on your job?	N	☐ 1	☐ 2	☐ 3	☐ 4	☐ 5
	L	☐ 1	☐ 2	☐ 3	☐ 4	☐ 5

Questions:

3. PROCEDURES
To what extent . . .

		1 To a very little extent	2 To a little extent	3 To some extent	4 To a good extent	5 To a great extent
A. Is information shared among the members of this team?	N	☐ 1	☐ 2	☐ 3	☐ 4	☐ 5
	L	☐ 1	☐ 2	☐ 3	☐ 4	☐ 5
B. Do members of this team plan and coordinate together?	N	☐ 1	☐ 2	☐ 3	☐ 4	☐ 5
	L	☐ 1	☐ 2	☐ 3	☐ 4	☐ 5

C. When decisions are made, are the persons affected asked for their ideas?	**N** **L**	☐ 1 ☐ 1	☐ 2 ☐ 2	☐ 3 ☐ 3	☐ 4 ☐ 4	☐ 5 ☐ 5
D. Do the members of this team make good decisions?	**N** **L**	☐ 1 ☐ 1	☐ 2 ☐ 2	☐ 3 ☐ 3	☐ 4 ☐ 4	☐ 5 ☐ 5
E. Are the team's meetings well run and productive?	**N** **L**	☐ 1 ☐ 1	☐ 2 ☐ 2	☐ 3 ☐ 3	☐ 4 ☐ 4	☐ 5 ☐ 5
F. Is communication during the meeting open and candid?	**N** **L**	☐ 1 ☐ 1	☐ 2 ☐ 2	☐ 3 ☐ 3	☐ 4 ☐ 4	☐ 5 ☐ 5
G. When conflict occurs in this team, do people look for collaborative solutions?	**N** **L**	☐ 1 ☐ 1	☐ 2 ☐ 2	☐ 3 ☐ 3	☐ 4 ☐ 4	☐ 5 ☐ 5
H. Does your team solve problems well?	**N** **L**	☐ 1 ☐ 1	☐ 2 ☐ 2	☐ 3 ☐ 3	☐ 4 ☐ 4	☐ 5 ☐ 5
I. Is your team well organized and efficient?	**N** **L**	☐ 1 ☐ 1	☐ 2 ☐ 2	☐ 3 ☐ 3	☐ 4 ☐ 4	☐ 5 ☐ 5
J. Do team members give each other feedback in a constructive, nonthreatening, direct way?	**N** **L**	☐ 1 ☐ 1	☐ 2 ☐ 2	☐ 3 ☐ 3	☐ 4 ☐ 4	☐ 5 ☐ 5
K. Do team members talk as a group about how they work together?	**N** **L**	☐ 1 ☐ 1	☐ 2 ☐ 2	☐ 3 ☐ 3	☐ 4 ☐ 4	☐ 5 ☐ 5
L. Does this team meet as a group?	**N** **L**	☐ 1 ☐ 1	☐ 2 ☐ 2	☐ 3 ☐ 3	☐ 4 ☐ 4	☐ 5 ☐ 5
M. Does this team need to meet often?	**N** **L**	☐ 1 ☐ 1	☐ 2 ☐ 2	☐ 3 ☐ 3	☐ 4 ☐ 4	☐ 5 ☐ 5

Questions:

4. RESOURCES To what extent . . .		**1** To a very little extent	**2** To a little extent	**3** To some extent	**4** To a good extent	**5** To a great extent
A. Do persons in this team know what their jobs are and know how to do them well?	N	☐ 1	☐ 2	☐ 3	☐ 4	☐ 5
	L	☐ 1	☐ 2	☐ 3	☐ 4	☐ 5
B. Do you now have adequate professional "updating" opportunities to keep you current in your field/function?	N	☐ 1	☐ 2	☐ 3	☐ 4	☐ 5
	L	☐ 1	☐ 2	☐ 3	☐ 4	☐ 5
C. Do you have information available to you to set objectives and monitor your performance?	N	☐ 1	☐ 2	☐ 3	☐ 4	☐ 5
	L	☐ 1	☐ 2	☐ 3	☐ 4	☐ 5
D. Is your team's physical space adequate, safe, and well maintained?	N	☐ 1	☐ 2	☐ 3	☐ 4	☐ 5
	L	☐ 1	☐ 2	☐ 3	☐ 4	☐ 5
E. Is your team's equipment adequate, safe, and well maintained?	N	☐ 1	☐ 2	☐ 3	☐ 4	☐ 5
	L	☐ 1	☐ 2	☐ 3	☐ 4	☐ 5
F. Are your team's tools adequate and well maintained?	N	☐ 1	☐ 2	☐ 3	☐ 4	☐ 5
	L	☐ 1	☐ 2	☐ 3	☐ 4	☐ 5
G. Do you have enough of the right materials at the right time to accomplish your team's goals and objectives?	N	☐ 1	☐ 2	☐ 3	☐ 4	☐ 5
	L	☐ 1	☐ 2	☐ 3	☐ 4	☐ 5
H. Does your team make the time to meet together?	N	☐ 1	☐ 2	☐ 3	☐ 4	☐ 5
	L	☐ 1	☐ 2	☐ 3	☐ 4	☐ 5

Questions:

5. PERFORMANCE To what extent . . .		**1** To a very little extent	**2** To a little extent	**3** To some extent	**4** To a good extent	**5** To a great extent
A. Are you pleased with the quality of your team's output?	N	☐ 1	☐ 2	☐ 3	☐ 4	☐ 5
	L	☐ 1	☐ 2	☐ 3	☐ 4	☐ 5
B. Are you pleased with the amount your team produces?	N	☐ 1	☐ 2	☐ 3	☐ 4	☐ 5
	L	☐ 1	☐ 2	☐ 3	☐ 4	☐ 5
C. Does your team meet its schedules for producing its outputs?	N	☐ 1	☐ 2	☐ 3	☐ 4	☐ 5
	L	☐ 1	☐ 2	☐ 3	☐ 4	☐ 5
D. Is the cost of your team output as low as possible?	N	☐ 1	☐ 2	☐ 3	☐ 4	☐ 5
	L	☐ 1	☐ 2	☐ 3	☐ 4	☐ 5
E. Is your team able to respond effectively to emergencies or unusual work demands placed on it?	N	☐ 1	☐ 2	☐ 3	☐ 4	☐ 5
	L	☐ 1	☐ 2	☐ 3	☐ 4	☐ 5
F. Are you satisfied with your team leader?	N	☐ 1	☐ 2	☐ 3	☐ 4	☐ 5
	L	☐ 1	☐ 2	☐ 3	☐ 4	☐ 5
G. Are you satisfied with your team members?	N	☐ 1	☐ 2	☐ 3	☐ 4	☐ 5
	L	☐ 1	☐ 2	☐ 3	☐ 4	☐ 5
H. Are you satisfied with your team rewards and compensation?	N	☐ 1	☐ 2	☐ 3	☐ 4	☐ 5
	L	☐ 1	☐ 2	☐ 3	☐ 4	☐ 5
I. Are you satisfied with your team members' contribution to achieving the team's goals?	N	☐ 1	☐ 2	☐ 3	☐ 4	☐ 5
	L	☐ 1	☐ 2	☐ 3	☐ 4	☐ 5

Questions:

6. RELATIONSHIPS To what extent . . .		**1** To a very little extent	**2** To a little extent	**3** To some extent	**4** To a good extent	**5** To a great extent
A. Are members of this team friendly and easy to approach?	N	☐ 1	☐ 2	☐ 3	☐ 4	☐ 5
	L	☐ 1	☐ 2	☐ 3	☐ 4	☐ 5
B. Is this team free from conflicts which could interfere with getting the work done?	N	☐ 1	☐ 2	☐ 3	☐ 4	☐ 5
	L	☐ 1	☐ 2	☐ 3	☐ 4	☐ 5
C. Is the team free from personal quarrels and disagreements?	N	☐ 1	☐ 2	☐ 3	☐ 4	☐ 5
	L	☐ 1	☐ 2	☐ 3	☐ 4	☐ 5
D. When you talk with persons in this team do they pay attention to what you are saying?	N	☐ 1	☐ 2	☐ 3	☐ 4	☐ 5
	L	☐ 1	☐ 2	☐ 3	☐ 4	☐ 5
E. Do you have confidence and trust in the members of this team?	N	☐ 1	☐ 2	☐ 3	☐ 4	☐ 5
	L	☐ 1	☐ 2	☐ 3	☐ 4	☐ 5
F. Do members have high morale and enthusiasm about working together in this team?	N	☐ 1	☐ 2	☐ 3	☐ 4	☐ 5
	L	☐ 1	☐ 2	☐ 3	☐ 4	☐ 5
G. Does the team meet informally to celebrate or socialize?	N	☐ 1	☐ 2	☐ 3	☐ 4	☐ 5
	L	☐ 1	☐ 2	☐ 3	☐ 4	☐ 5

Questions:

7. ORGANIZATION To what extent . . .		**1** To a very little extent	**2** To a little extent	**3** To some extent	**4** To a good extent	**5** To a great extent
A. Is your team rewarded for excellent performance?	N	☐ 1	☐ 2	☐ 3	☐ 4	☐ 5
	L	☐ 1	☐ 2	☐ 3	☐ 4	☐ 5
B. Does your organization support and encourage your working as a team?	N	☐ 1	☐ 2	☐ 3	☐ 4	☐ 5
	L	☐ 1	☐ 2	☐ 3	☐ 4	☐ 5
C. Does the organization support your team in resolving conflicts that may exist with other teams in the organization?	N	☐ 1	☐ 2	☐ 3	☐ 4	☐ 5
	L	☐ 1	☐ 2	☐ 3	☐ 4	☐ 5

5. ROLE DEFINITION DEVELOPMENT

The clarity of a role definition is a fundamental requirement to optimize individual performance, increase job satisfaction, value-add as a team member, and maximize one's role/function in the value chain. It is the underpinning of a performance management system. This process will assist in eliminating role conflict between individuals, as well as role ambiguity for each person, resulting in increased effectiveness and efficiency. **Pay particular attention to how this process works.**

Start with the following **Role Analysis Worksheet** below with the section describing your present "As Is" role.

Then, before going on to the "Should Be" role definition portion, which starts on page 194, have meaningful discussions about your "As Is" answers with your board, supervisor, peers, and subordinates. Next, examine the example of a completed "Should Be" role definition before you complete the blank role definition template.

At the end of this exercise, the Discussion Points (page 196) will help to finalize an accurate role definition. Keep in mind that this role definition process will assist to evolve your role and others from an "As Is" to a "Should Be" status.

Role Analysis Worksheet

Describe your present "As Is" role definition

I.   Job title: _____

II.   Report to: _____

III.   Number of people reporting to you (list):

_____

_____

_____

_____

_____

_____

IV.   What is your primary function?

_____

_____

_____

_____

_____

_____

V.   List the five most significant responsibilities of this job:

_____

_____

_____

_____

_____

_____

VI. How is your time spent? List up to ten activities. Of the 100 percent of time available, approximately what percent of time is devoted to each activity?

Activity	% of Total Time
1. _____	_____
2. _____	_____
3. _____	_____
4. _____	_____
5. _____	_____
6. _____	_____
7. _____	_____
8. _____	_____
9. _____	_____
10. _____	_____

VII. What skills are most needed to perform this job successfully?

A. Technical skills:

_____

_____

_____

_____

_____

_____

B. Nontechnical (intra- and interpersonal) skills:

_____

_____

_____

_____

_____

_____

VIII. What support from others is most needed to perform this job successfully?

A. Technical support:

_____

_____

_____

_____

_____

_____

B. Nontechnical support:

_____

_____

_____

_____

_____

_____

IX. What equipment and/or resources are required to perform this job successfully? What equipment and/or resources are you lacking?

_____

_____

_____

_____

_____

_____

X. What currently are the greatest obstacles or difficulties in performing this job successfully?

_____

_____

_____

_____

_____

_____

XI. Please itemize what decisions you are responsible for in your normal daily activities. What are the limitations of your decision-making authority?

_____

_____

_____

_____

_____

_____

_____

XII. Please identify decisions that you believe should be your sole responsibility, which currently are not:

_____

_____

_____

_____

_____

XIII. Please identify, in your best judgment, specific decisions currently being made by the "wrong" person that you believe should be made by you or others, in light of perceived strengths and weaknesses (people skills/technical skills):

_____

_____

_____

_____

_____

_____

_____

_____

_____

XIV. Time allocations:

Responsibilities/Objectives	% of Total Time
1. _____	_____
2. _____	_____
3. _____	_____
4. _____	_____
5. _____	_____
6. _____	_____
7. _____	_____
8. _____	_____

Example of a completed "Should Be" role definition

I.   **Name:** Steve Wick

II. **Title:** Vice President, Director of Marketing and Sales

III. **Reports to:** David Gerringer, CEO

IV. **Individuals reporting into this function:**
  - Administrative assistant
  - Service and installation manager
  - Sales and marketing regional representatives (3)
  - Overseas representatives for Europe and Asia (3)

V. Basic Function:

To develop and lead a strategic marketing and sales function, which will assure that annual sales goals are achieved in support of the company's annual strategic business plan, including its current strategy, financial and market assumptions, and goals.

VI. Critical Responsibilities:

  A. Existing/new customer relationships for automotive

    ○ Maintain, improve, and expand relationships with current/ new customers to achieve annual sales goal

  B. Marketing and sales for new design machinery worldwide

    ○ Expand sales of machinery to aerospace/nuclear power industries to achieve annual sales and revenue goals

  C. Marketing and Sales Function Management

    ○ Develop and present annual M&S plan for ratification and execution for planning year

    ○ Manage marketing and sales staff with a defined management/ accountability process

    ○ Develop relationships and manage sales representatives in nonlocal/state geographical areas to expand company sales

  D. Product and Services Development

    ○ R&D staff interface to provide feedback of specific customer requirements and suggestions

    ○ Inform R&D staff of competitors' offerings and strengths and weaknesses

    ○ Coordinate/assist CEO and CFO in products/services mix development and pricing

  E. Customer Service Requirement Management

    ○ Coordinate project management for large design equipment sales

    ○ Help coordinate installation and service based on customer requests

- Provide consistent and formal customer feedback to production, engineering, service departments, and CEO

F. Leadership and Team Development

- Support CEO to build the core team with existing and new members utilizing a uniform role-definition template
- Affirm/support the core team to build strong and self-managed departments
- Have a monthly work, planning, and review session with CEO
- Build a high-performance M&S team utilizing Five Dysfunctions team model
- Develop M&S strategy/plan for the sales department that will drive the company to reach its annual sales/revenue goal and to provide a path toward succession for this department

VII. **Improvement Objectives:** What are the improvement objectives you will achieve to increase your role effectiveness?

A. Technical

- Professional sales training to improve price negotiation and sales closings
- Become better organized with documents, both physical and electronic

B. Intra-/interpersonal

- Make and commit to decisions quicker with less procrastination and more self-accountability
- Practice leadership and management skills (i.e., coaching, evaluating, empowering) including formal team-building processes
- Interface with internal departments more effectively (i.e., self-confidence, emotional self-control, self-awareness, empathy, and social awareness)
- Learn how to administer performance evaluations/coaching sessions (WPR) for my team members

VIII. Time allocations: Responsibilities/Objectives (Based on 160 hours per month)

Responsibilities/Objectives	% of Total Time
Research, network, and sell to new machine design customers to achieve monthly sales goals	25
Selling to existing/new machine design customers to achieve monthly sales goals	25
Strategy development and participation in design/ engineering and quality improvement processes with production and engineering	15
Brand/company ambassador to improve company image to customers, employees, and suppliers, including website development	10
Assisting sales staff and making decisions regarding products/ services, prices, geographic regions, and new markets	15
M&S leadership/team development and core team development/participation, CEO monthly WPR session	5
Project management for new machines installations	5

Role Definition: "Should Be" Template

I. Name: _____

II. Title: _____

III. Report to: _____

IV. Individuals (names) reporting into this function:

_____

_____

_____

_____

V. Basic function:

_____

_____

_____

_____

VI. Critical responsibilities:

_____

_____

_____

_____

_____

_____

_____

_____

VII. Improvement objectives:

What are the improvement objectives you will achieve to increase your role effectiveness?

A. Technical:

_____

_____

_____

_____

B. Intra-/interpersonal:

_____

_____

_____

_____

VIII. Time allocations:

Responsibilities/Objectives	% of Total Time
1. _____	_____
2. _____	_____
3. _____	_____
4. _____	_____
5. _____	_____
6. _____	_____
7. _____	_____
8. _____	_____

Role Definition Discussion Points

- Does the basic function fit the title?
- Is there clarity in the reporting relationship?
- What should be "the best" reporting relationship to service both external and internal customers?
- Do the critical responsibilities belong in this role or should they be in another role and/or individual?
- Do you have enough time to effectively discharge your responsibilities? If not, what suggestion(s) do you have?
- What technical skills (e.g., customer relationship management, marketing, brand development, market analysis) should be emphasized for this role to be successfully executed?
- What interpersonal skills and attitudes (e.g., listening, problem solving, conflict resolution, consensus building, social awareness, empathy, closing skills) should be emphasized for this role to be successfully executed?

6. TEAM DEVELOPMENT EXERCISE MODULE

Emotional Intelligence (EI) Assessment

Emotional intelligence is the ability to integrate feeling and thinking to make better choices and optimize decision making. Being "intelligent with feelings" is essential to effective leading and managing—building engagement, navigating challenge, and accelerating change. The skills of emotional intelligence have practical applications in numerous areas of organizational and professional performance. The EI terminology/nomenclature will be helpful for you to define and be more concise with your thoughts. It is a vocabulary that you can adopt for future discussions. But more important, this self-assessment will be useful to discuss the challenges and opportunities of increasing emotional intelligence for our individual roles, teams, and workplace. Other objectives of this developmental session are to increase team trust, encourage us to step into the fear of conflict, and embolden our emotional commitment to the team. We can practice and learn together.

Please review the EI capabilities that follow—as defined by Daniel Goleman—and respond to the following statements.

1. In the **Personal Competence** section (how we manage ourselves), please identify for yourself:
   A. One strength
   B. One weakness
   C. One blind spot (what others see that you don't). Take a guess.
2. In the **Social Competence** section (how we manage others), please identify for yourself:
   A. One strength
   B. One weakness
   C. One blind spot (what others see that you don't). Take a guess.

3. Now you will share your self-assessment and receive group feedback. Your other team members will have the opportunity to think through questions 1 and 2 and jot down their responses before you share your results. The group feedback will be a significant opportunity for you to find out how you are perceived, in a safe and trusting place called your team.

Note: You may feel stymied by "guessing/predicting" something you cannot see. Have some fun; again, take a guess, and go with the flow. You may be surprised after receiving your feedback to realize you know yourself better than you thought.

Personal Competence

These capabilities determine how we manage ourselves:

- Self-Awareness
  - *Emotional self-awareness*: Reading one's own emotions and recognizing their impact; using "gut sense" to guide decisions
  - *Accurate self-assessment*: Knowing one's own strengths and limits
  - *Self-confidence*: A sound sense of one's self-worth and capabilities

- Self-Management
  - *Emotional self-control*: Keeping disruptive emotions and impulses under control
  - *Transparency*: Displaying honesty and integrity; trustworthiness
  - *Adaptability*: Flexibility in adapting to changing situations or overcoming obstacles

- ○ *Achievement*: The drive to improve performance to meet inner standards of excellence
- ○ *Initiative*: Readiness to act and seize opportunities
- ○ *Optimism*: Seeing the upside in events

Social Competence

These capabilities determine how we manage relationships:

- Social Awareness
    - ○ *Empathy*: Sensing others' emotions, understanding their perspective, and taking active interest in their concerns
    - ○ *Organizational awareness*: Reading the current decision networks and politics at the organizational level
    - ○ *Service*: Recognizing and meeting follower, client, or customer needs

- Relationship Management
    - ○ *Inspirational leadership*: Guiding and motivating with a compelling vision
    - ○ *Influence*: Wielding a range of tactics for persuasion
    - ○ *Developing others*: Bolstering others' abilities through feedback and guidance
    - ○ *Change catalyst*: Initiating, managing, and leading in a new direction
    - ○ *Conflict management*: Resolving disagreements
    - ○ *Teamwork and collaboration*: Cooperation and team building[1]

Session Debriefing/Future Applications/
Individual Commitments/Next Steps

1. We have gone through a significant experience together. What are your feelings and thoughts?
2. What was the most impactful part of this session? Why?
3. Moving forward, how may we utilize what was captured in today's session (i.e., personal improvement objectives)?
4. What one improvement objective do you want to commit to and share with your team, as you include this assessment and feedback for improvement objectives into your current role?
5. What should the next steps be, to make sure we follow through on our commitments?

7. STRATEGIC ISSUE DEFINITION, GOAL STATEMENT, AND OBJECTIVES/ACTION STEPS

I. **Strategic Issue:**

Marketing & Sales

II. **Issue Definition:**

The absence of more accurate marketing and sales plans, a clear mission, competitive advantage, competitive intelligence, and a formal strategy creates inconsistency and confusion in the company and marketplace. This impacts ABC's competitive/market posture, negatively impacting top-line revenue and profitability.

III. **Goal Statement:**

To achieve ABC's annual top-line revenue goal and to impact profitability by eliminating confusion and inconsistency inside the company and in the marketplace by formalizing M&S plans, increasing departmental effectiveness/efficiency, and developing mission, competitive advantage statements, competitive analysis, and a strategic narrative by year-end 12.31.20.

Champion: Dick Ryan   Co-Champion: Peter Dexter

IV. Objectives/Action Step	Person(s)	Date
A. Sales and Marketing Plans: To complete both plans tied into 2020 budget/forecast	Dick Peter Tony Henry	4/30/20
B. Functional/Fitness Assessment: M&S Department to assess itself through a SWOT analysis including roles; and develop objectives for fitness, departmental, and role improvements	Same Owners Management team	7/31/20
C. Mission Statement: To formulate a current and relevant corporate mission statement comprising the assessment of current customer needs, products and services, and delivery standards and present to owners and the management team (MT) for ratification.	Same	9/30/20
D. Competitive Advantage Statement: To formulate a competitive advantage statement presented to the owners and the MT for ratification.	Same	9/30/20
E. Competitive analyses: To complete a competitive analysis by identifying and comparing ABC to its top ten competitors to verify our competitive advantage and support our sales/marketing/branding plans to the owners and MT for ratification.	Same	10/31/20
F. Strategy Formation: To complete a strategy narrative utilizing (A–E), which will serve to drive the 5-year strategic vision to be presented to the owner and the MT for ratification.	Same	11/30/20
G. Goal/Action Plan Assessment: To assess the 2020 issue/goal/objective's plan and extend action plan for year-end 2021 if necessary	Champion Co-Champion Management Team	Year-End Retreat

8. GOAL/ACTION PLAN TEAM RATIFICATION SESSION

I.   Goal: _____

II. Champion/Coordinator: _____

III. Assessment Criteria

1	2	3	4

Not clear and poorly articulated	Very clear and well articulated
Lacking thoroughness and comprehensiveness	Thorough and comprehensive
Not complete/drop-dead dates unrealistic	Complete/drop-dead dates realistic
Champion not motivated	Champion highly motivated
Champion not realistic	Champion realistic
Champion not empowered	Champion empowered
Champion not self-managed	Champion self-managed
Reactive	Proactive
Low execution	High execution

IV. Assessment Score:

On a 1–4 scale, 4 being the highest, I feel this action plan is rated at a
_____ for the following reasons:
SCORE

_____

_____

_____

_____

_____

_____

_____

V.　Action plan recommendations, additions, and considerations in order for this plan to receive a "4" ratification score:

_____

_____

_____

_____

APPENDIX SUMMARY

The Appendix items, along with the full text of the book, point you toward the true line of leadership posture. If you were my client, we would go on from this point to develop a personalized and prioritized coaching regimen, with periodic sessions for assessment, setting new objectives and guidance, all within the framework and context of your company's current strategy and goals. But even without such a coaching relationship, you can employ what you have discovered about where you and your business stand now and use those findings to move toward an Alignment Strong organization.

Notes

Preface

1. Robert M. Pirsig, *Zen and the Art of Motorcycle Maintenance* (New York: William Morrow, 2005).
2. Jack Kornfield, *A Path with Heart* (New York: Bantam, 1993).

Introduction

1. Debra Adelaide, *The Australian* (Weekend edition), February 18–19, 2012.

Chapter 1

1. Denison Consulting, Denison Volume 7, Issue 2 (Ann Arbor, MI: 2012); www.denisonconsulting.com.

Chapter 2

1. Thomas McGuane, *Ninety-Two in the Shade* (New York: Farrar, Straus & Giroux, 1973).
2. *Poems of Rumi*, translated by Coleman Barks, The Threshold Society, 2016; sufism.org/origins/rumi/rumi-excerpts/poems-of-rumi-tr-by-coleman-barks-published-by-threshold-books-2.
3. Catherine Fitzgerald and Jennifer Garvey Berger, *Executive Coaching: Practices & Perspectives* (Boston: Nicholas Brealey, 2002).

4. Alfred Adler, *Understanding Human Nature* (London: Oneworld Publications, 1992).

5. John P. Kotter, *Leading Change* (Boston: Harvard Business Review Press, 1996).

6. Roger L. Martin, "The Big Lie of Strategic Planning," *Harvard Business Review*, January–February 2014.

7. Edgar Schein, *Helping: How to Offer, Give, and Receive Help* (Berret-Koehler Publishers, 2009).

8. Leon F. Seltzer, "You Only Get More of What You Resist–Why?" *Psychology Today* , June 2015, https://www.psychologytoday.com/us/blog/evolution-the-self/201606/you-only-get-more-what-you-resist-why.

9. Korn Ferry Institute, "The Effectiveness of Executive Coaching: What We Can Learn from Research Literature," 2009.

Chapter 3

1. Patrick Lencioni, *The Five Dysfunctions of a Team* (Hoboken, NJ: Jossey-Bass, 2002).

2. T. E. Deal and A. A. Kennedy, *Corporate Cultures: The Rites and Rituals of Corporate Life* (Boston: Addison-Wesley, 1982).

3. Peter F. Drucker, *Management: Tasks, Responsibilities, Practices* (New York: Harper & Row, 1974).

4. Ibid.

5. Ibid.

6. W. Chan Kim and Renée Mauborgne, *Blue Ocean Strategy* (Boston: Harvard Business Review Press, 2004, revised edition 2015).

7. W. Chan Kim and Renée Mauborgne, "How to Achieve Resilient Growth Throughout the Business Cycle," *Harvard Business Review*, March 2020.

8. Daniel Goleman, Richard Boyatzis, and Annie McKee, *Primal Leadership: Unleashing the Power of Emotional Intelligence* (Boston: Harvard Business Review Press, 2016).

9. Bjorn Christian Martinoff and Victoria Penaflor Martinoff, *Unstoppable: Leadership and Exponential Results* (F1C International, 2018).

10. James Kouzes and Barry Posner, *Credibility: How Leaders Gain and Lose It, Why People Demand It* (San Francisco: Jossey-Bass, 1993).

11. David L. Dotlich and Peter C. Cairo, *Why CEOs Fail* (San Francisco: Jossey-Bass, 2003).

12. Colin Horn, PhD, "Types of Power and Their Manifestations," 1999.

13. Daniel Goleman and Richard Boyatzi, "Social Intelligence and the Biology of Leadership," *Harvard Business Review*, September 2008, https://hbr.org/2008/09/social-intelligence-and-the-biology-of-leadership.

14. Michael Schneider, "Google Spent 2 Years Studying 180 Teams. The Most Successful Ones Shared These 5 Traits," *Inc.*, July 19, 2017. https://www.inc.com/michael-schneider/google-thought-they-knew-how-to-create-the-perfect.html.

15. Sidney Yoshida's 1989 study, "The Iceberg of Ignorance."

16. Joan Magretta, *Understanding Michael Porter: The Essential Guide to Competition and Strategy* (Boston: Harvard Business Review Press, 2012).

17. Ibid.

18. Henry Mintzberg, *Strategy Safari: A Guided Tour Through the Wilds of Strategic Management* (New York: Free Press, 1998).

19. Joan Magretta, *Understanding Michael Porter: The Essential Guide to Competition and Strategy* (Boston: Harvard Business Review Press, 2012).

20. Robert S. Kaplan and David P. Norton, "Mastering the Management System," *Harvard Business Review*, January 2008, https://hbr.org/2008/01/mastering-the-management-system.

21. Michael E Porter, "The Five Competitive Forces That Shape Strategy," *Harvard Business Review*, January 2008, Volume 88, No. 1, pp 78–93.

22. Gary Latham and Gary Yukl, "A Review of Research on the Application of Goal Setting in Organizations," *Academy of Management Journal* (1975).

23. Marshall Sashkin, *A Manager's Guide to Participative Management* (New York: Amacom Books, 1982).

24. Robert H. Schaffer, *High-Impact Consulting: How Clients and Consultants Can Work Together to Achieve Extraordinary Results* (Hoboken, NJ: Jossey-Bass, 2002).

25. Ibid.

26. Nedal M. Elsaid, Ahmed E. Okasha, and Abdalla A. Abdelghaly, "Defining and Solving the Organizational Structure Problems to Improve the Performance of Ministry of State for Environmental Affairs—Egypt," *International Journal of Scientific and Research Publications*, vol. 3, issue 10, October 2013.

27. Michael Hammer, *The Agenda: What Every Business Must Do to Dominate the Decade* (New York: Crown Business, 2001).

28. Peter Cappelli and Anna Tavis, "The Performance Management Revolution," *Harvard Business Review*, October 2016. https://hbr.org/2016/10/the-performance-management-revolution.

29. Catherine Fitzgerald and Jennifer Garvey Berger, *Executive Coaching: Practices & Perspectives* (Boston: Nicholas Brealey, 2002).

30. Daniel Goleman, "Leadership That Gets Results," *Harvard Business Review*, March 2000.

31. Denison Consulting, Denison Volume 7, Issue 2 (Ann Arbor, MI: 2012); www.denisonconsulting.com.

32. Max De Pree, *Leadership Is an Art* (Michigan State University Press: 1987; reprinted by Currency Doubleday, 1989).

33. James Joyce, *Finnegans Wake* (New York: Penguin Classics, reissue edition 1999).

Chapter 5

1. *As Others See Us: A Look at Interpersonal Relationships* (video), Salenger Educational Media (1981).

2. Philip K. Dick, *A Scanner Darkly* (Boston: Mariner Books, 2011).

3. Jim Haudan and Rich Berens, *What Are Your Blind Spots? Conquering the 5 Misconceptions that Hold Leaders Back* (New York: McGraw-Hill, 2018).

4. Daniel Goleman, *Emotional Intelligence* (London: Bloomsbury, 1995).

5. Monty Roberts, *The Man Who Listens to Horses* (New York: Random House, 1997).

6. Henri J. M. Nouwen, *Show Me the Way* (Spring Valley, NY: Crossroad, 1992).

7. Aldous Huxley, *Texts and Pretexts: An Anthology with Commentaries* (London: Chatto & Windus, 1932).

Chapter 6

1. Anne Rød and Marita Fridjhon, *Creating Intelligent Teams* (Bryanston, South Africa: KR Publishing, 2016).

2. Don Beck and Christopher Cowan, *Spiral Dynamics* (Hoboken, NJ: Wiley-Blackwell, 2005).

3. Patrick Lencioni, *The Five Dysfunctions of a Team* (Hoboken, NJ: Jossey-Bass, 2002).

4. Carol S. Dweck, *Mindset: The New Psychology of Success* (New York: Random House, 2006).

5. Ibid.

6. Ibid.

7. Ibid.

8. Herbert Fingarette, *The Self in Transformation: Psychoanalysis, Philosophy and the Life of the Spirit* (New York: Harper Torchbooks, 1965).

Chapter 7

1. Laura Sherbin and Ripa Rashid, "Diversity Doesn't Stick Without Inclusion," *Harvard Business Review*, February 2017. https://hbr.org/2017/02/diversity-doesnt-stick-without-inclusion.

2. Paul Zak, "The Neuroscience of Trust," *Harvard Business Review*, January–February 2017; https://hbr.org/2017/01/the-neuroscience-of-trust.

3. Robert Putnam, *Bowling Alone: The Collapse and Revival of American Community* (New York: Touchstone Books, 2001).

4. Emanuele Ferragina, *Social Capital in Europe: A Comparative Regional Analysis* (Cheltenham, UK: Edward Elgar, 2012).

Appendix

1. Daniel Goleman, Richard E. Boyatzis, and Annie McKee, *Primal Leadership: Realizing the Power of Emotional Intelligence* (Boston: Harvard Business Review Press, 2002).

Index

About the Author

John Quinlan, a co-founder, chairman, and CEO of a publicly traded financial services holding company, guided his organization, with his two brothers, from inception to 320 employees occupying 28 offices in 14 states and $430 million in assets. Quinlan ended up losing it all. Returning to graduate school, he received a master of science degree in organization development. Integrating this knowledge with his financial background, he co-established his own consulting and investment banking firm in Detroit, Michigan. He then left America for Papua New Guinea, where he founded, with his wife, Fiona, a certified-organic and Rainforest Alliance coffee growing, collection, and exporting business. Ultimately, local greed and vengeance, culminating in an assassination attempt, forced the Quinlans to abandon their company. John's first book, *Tau Bada: The Quest and Memoir of a Vulnerable Man*, describes this adventure and led to a TEDx talk, "Journey into Vulnerability: Lessons from a Rainforest CEO." *Inc.* magazine's Patrick Hainault, vice president of corporate business development, commented, "John Quinlan is an entrepreneurial polymath with a depth and breadth of experiences few can match." Quinlan is now an author, speaker, organization development specialist, and executive leadership coach. He holds a Bachelor of Arts in Economics from Albion College in Michigan, and a Master of Science in Organizational Development (MSOD) from the American University, Washington, D.C.